Natchez:

The History
& Mystery
of the
City on the Bluff

by

Mitchel Whitington

ENJOY THESE TALES OF NATCHEZ !

[signature]

ISBN
0-9801850-2-5 (10 digit)
978-0-9801850-2-7 (13 digit)

Library of Congress Catalog Number: 2008906671

First Edition

Printed in the United States of America
Published by 23 House Publishing
SAN 299-8084
www.23house.com

This book is dedicated to
Natchez' most
enthusiastic ambassadors
and my good friends
Mike & Lisa Barry

Thank you so much
for all the help and inspiration,
and for introducing me
to the many wonders of
the City on the Bluff!

And a Special Thanks To...

Ginnie Siena Bivona for all the help, encouragement, and downright nagging to get the book finished. Also for prying the comma key off my keyboard, and barring me from using the word "however" for life.

Leonard & Betty Whitington, my parents, for kindly suffering through the raw read of yet another book; as always, your love and support means everything to me.

Ann Tillman for sharing a year of her life with us while this book was being written, and for many valued comments on the manuscript.

Kirk & Judy Bartley for the location of the Devil's Punchbowl, a great evening at The Castle Pub, and giving me a native's read of the manuscript.

Ron & Mimi Miller, wonderful champions of the city, innkeepers supreme, and our hosts for most every trip that we've made to Natchez... see you soon, guys.

The curator of the Rodney Church – I wish that I could remember your name, because you were great!

Jacqueline & Robert Stephens, former proprietors of the Natchez Ghost Walk and all-around nice people.

All the wonderful people of Natchez who answered questions, told stories, and gave me information for this book. You're far too numerous to name, but you all have my eternal thanks.

...and always, to my loving wife Tami, who makes this life worth living. I love you.

Table of Contents

An Introduction To Natchez

Natchez, Mississippi, is truly a city with which you will fall in love. This grand old belle of the South simply exudes pageantry, passion, history, and glamour. Some of its visitors are immediately smitten, and are drawn into the city to spend their lives there. Others form a life-long, flirtatious bond, first coming to Pilgrimage, then to various holidays, to other celebrations and festivals, and finally just looking for any reason or excuse to escape to the city on the bluff.

There is literally something in Natchez for everyone, whether you are seeking out an antique table to fill an empty space in your home, or stalking the perfect steak, grilled to perfection. You will find a rousing football-watching party in many of the taverns on a chilly fall evening, or you can take a carriage ride around the town to learn of its history and

1

romance. Whether you live in Natchez, or only visit there regularly, the city will carve out a niche for itself in your heart.

So how does one introduce such a place? Is it best to tell of the huge mammoths roaming the countryside eons ago, or begin with the stories of the Native Americans that gave the city its name? There is no easy answer – Natchez is like an old patchwork quilt that has been handed down through many generations of a family. You'll find rough spots and smooth places, maybe a few that are threadbare and others that have been mended, but when you step back and view it as a whole, it can only be described as "beautiful."

I love talking about Natchez, but this introduction was the last thing that I wrote for the book – I'd been putting it off, because I had no idea how to sum up the city in a single introductory chapter. My answer came when I realized that it couldn't be done; this entire book is about the city, and weaves its story from the beginning of time until present day.

I discovered that fact while talking to some of the visitors to the city – where else in the world could you find a tourist that could tell you so much: what homes would be on the Spring Pilgrimage tour, where the Historic Natchez Pageant Queen has registered for her china, and who was playing at Bowie's Tavern next weekend. I promise you, it's easy to find that person in Natchez, because people keep coming back, and back, and back again.

It's true; people fall in love with this town, and they become residents *in absentia*.

It is for those folks that this book is written – it is a love letter from me to the city of which I have become so enamored. There were items that took me years to research, and decisions that had to be made about what went in and what was left out with which I still struggle. The houses that I included, for example, are all places that you can visit year-round, either as an operating tour home or a B&B – this meant leaving out some other grand old homes, and it pained me to do so, but I

2

wanted you to be able to experience the places that I wrote about for yourself.

Some things, such as the story of the Barber of Natchez, will make many residents smile. Others, like the fact that I mentioned a little woman named Miss Nellie, might make a few of the people a little uncomfortable. But Natchez really is, as I pointed out earlier, a patchwork quilt. The best thing about that is, at the end of the day, you can pull it up around you and fall into a sleep filled with dreams of years gone by... and I hope that this book helps you in that regard. If it does, then I have done my duty as an author and a fan of this wonderful old city.

All that said, come with me on a journey though Natchez' past, and learn the history and mystery of the city on the bluff...

The City's Namesake — The Natchez Indians

The story of this grand old town begins long ago, before Europeans had ever set foot on North American soil.

The Natchez Indians occupied the lower Mississippi River Valley; archaeological evidence indicates that their culture began around 700 A.D. They were a generally peaceful people, although some of their practices might seem barbaric to us today. The Natchez were accomplished farmers, hunters and fishermen.

Anthropologists studying their language believe that the Natchez developed from earlier cultures in the Lower Mississippi River Valley, because they spoke a dialect with ties to the Muskogean language.

The Natchez society was a monarchy, or more specifically,

a chiefdom. The ruler of the tribe had absolute say over all aspects of life. The people were divided into two classes: commoners and nobility. Position in a class was determined by heredity through the female line, which is known as matrilineal descent. Basically, if you mother was a commoner, so were you... no matter who your father might have been.

The Great Sun's Mount at the Grand Village of the Natchez

They were also mound-builders – in other words, they constructed large mounds of dirt to lift their sacred buildings closer to the sky. All members of the tribe worked together to build and maintain the flat-topped, ceremonial mounds. The rulers of the cities were the only ones to live there on a permanent basis. Within their homes were the bones of the deceased Chiefs, contained in boxes and baskets. Three logs of wood joined at the ends and placed in a triangle, occupied the middle part of the floor, and burned slowly away, night and

5

day. Keepers attended and constantly removed them.

The common people of the tribe were spread over a wide area surrounding the mounds, where they gathered for special religious and social activities.

The Natchez Indians worshipped the sun, and believing that their rulers were descendents from that celestial body. The chiefs of the Natchez cities were called "Suns," and the head chief of the Natchez nation was called the "Great Sun." Every morning, as the sun appeared on the horizon, the chief would stand at the doorway of his cabin on the mound, turn his face toward the east, and bow three times, at the same time prostrating himself on the ground. A pipe – which was never lighted in leisure – was handed to him. He would then puff smoke, first toward the Sun, and then toward the other three quarters of the horizon. It was a ritual that brought blessings onto his people.

When the Great Sun died, all of his guards and attendants were obliged to follow him in death to the spirit world, as were his close friends and relations. The ceremonies to send these others on their path to the other side have often been chronicled as barbaric human sacrifices, but in reality, the positions were greatly sought after. This "other side" was a place of abundance, where those inhabitants who were good of heart, mind and spirit enjoyed a continual feast of venison, corn, melons and other worldly delights. Those who were bad found themselves condemned to an eternity of spoiled fish and rotten food. Escorting the Great Sun would ensure prosperity on the other side, though, so the death of a chief could involve the voluntary deaths of over one hundred persons.

Upon his death, the Great Sun was succeeded by the son of his nearest female relative, who was called the "Woman Chief." Although she did not share in the ruling of the tribe, she was given great honors; the death of a Woman Chief was very similar to that of the Great Sun, including the accompanying of her spirit by her guards and attendants.

6

The chief and his family did not work the land; instead, periodic festivals were held where the tribe members would bring food and supplies in tribute to their leader.

The Natchez' Emerald Mound

The Jesuit explorer Pierre F.X. de Charlevoix visited the Natchez Indians and described their temple by saying that he, "Never saw anything more slovenly and dirty, nor more in disorder... We see nothing in their outward appearance that distinguishes them from the other savages of Canada and Louisiana. They seldom make war, not placing their glory in destroying men. What distinguishes them more particularly is the form of their government, entirely despotic; a great dependence, which extends even to a kind of slavery in the subjects; more pride and grandeur in the chiefs and their pacific spirit, which, however, they have not entirely preserved for some years past."

7

While his words may seem harsh, he did observe some extremely interesting things. For example, he pointed out that, "They seldom make war, not placing their glory in destroying men." That itself seems like a noble accolade. When Charlevoix describes them as slaves, he is actually commenting on the commoner's devotion to their ruling class, which could just as easily be seen in early Britain. From all indications, the Natchez Indians had an orderly, peaceful, religious existence.

The Museum at the Grand Village of the Natchez

The Emerald Mound, located about ten miles from Natchez on the Natchez Trace Parkway, was probably the main ceremonial mound during the period of 1200-1600 A.D. After that, the main tribal center shifted to the Grand Village of the Natchez, situated along St. Catherine's Creek, which is now a preserved historical park.

When first visited by the French in 1682, the Natchez

8

numbered around 6,000 people spread out in over fifty settlements. Little did they know the fate that awaited them... but that is a story for later.

Today, you can visit the Grand Village of the Natchez and see not only their ceremonial mounds, but also a museum of their culture.

Grand Village of the Natchez
400 Jefferson Davis Blvd
Natchez, MS 39120
601.446.6502

The French Arrive, and The Natchez Massacre

Robert de LaSalle

The Spanish explorer Hernando de Soto came to this area in 1541 while searching for gold. Over a hundred years later, in 1682, the Frenchman René Robert Cavelier, Sieur de La Salle, or simply Robert de LaSalle, ventured through while he was following the Mississippi River. He claimed the land and named it "Louisiana," in honor of King Louis XIV. The first French settlement was established near Biloxi, Mississippi, in the year 1699 by d'Iberville, who landed on the Gulf Coast and initiated trade with the Natchez people. A second settlement was founded in 1716 by Jean Baptiste le Moyne de Bienville – brother of d'Iberville – at Fort Rosalie, in the location that is now the City of Natchez. While the settlement continued to grow, disputes between the French and the Natchez Indians were common, although on the surface relations seemed to be going well.

The first problem between the Natchez Indians and outsiders occurred in 1716, and as such, became to be known as the "Incident of 1716." The Natchez had been putting up with the French for quite some time, and grew weary of dealing with them and their strange ways. It all came to a culmination when four Natchez braves robbed and murdered four French fur traders. Governor Antoine de Lamothe Cadillac ordered de Bienville and the military to get the Natchez Indians under control. When Bienville demanded that the Natchez Indians turn over the guilty parties, the Natchez sent the heads of four Caucasian men. Bienville, commander of Fort Rosalie, took a force of forty-nine men out to resolve the problem, and they captured the Natchez' "Great Sun" and other leaders, whom they threatened with capital punishment.

The Natchez finally sent the heads of the four guilty parties to the fort, in addition to the innocent men they had already slain. The Great Sun and other leaders were released. Unfortunately, relations between the Natchez Indians and the French went spiraling downhill from there.

Fort Rosalie grew, as did the outlying areas. Plantations began to spring up in the area, crowding out the Natchez Indians more and more.

The command of Fort Rosalie was transferred from Bienville to Sieur de Chopart, a man with a dastardly reputation. He took the position with a plan to claim more land for France, even though it was occupied by the Natchez Indians, and included their sacred mounds.

When Chopart's intentions became obvious, the Natchez laid plans to stop the French.

On November 18th, 1729, the Natchez Indians set out with a plan of attack. They convinced de Chopart that the men of the tribe were about to debark on a massive hunting trip and needed to trade for powder and lead.

De Chopart believed the story and permitted the Natchez to enter the fort. The Great Sun, leader of the Indians, told de Chopart that his people had wild game and corn for trade. The Indians spread the bounty out on the floor and de Chopart stooped down to examine the meat and produce. As he did, the Natchez opened fire, killing him.

The Great Sun walked out into the courtyard of the fort and sat down in the shade to let the events of the day play out. A massacre ensued. The French people who were fortunate, or perhaps just lucky, died quickly at the first of the attack,

11

because many were simply captured and then tortured to death. As the Great Sun sat watching the butchery, his warriors decapitated the Frenchmen and started constructing a pyramid out of their heads. De Chopart's was placed at the pinnacle of the gruesome pile. Out of Fort Roaslie's five hundred residents, only twenty-five men lived to tell of the slaughter. The bodies were left out in the sun as food for the vultures and other predators. The fort itself was put to the torch, leaving the once-proud outpost of the French as a vestige of ashes and blood.

Little did the Indians know that their victory would be very short-lived. A couple of the French soldiers had been out hunting, and returned to see the aftermath of the Natchez attack – they managed to escape and quickly made their way down to New Orleans where they told the fateful story of Fort Rosalie.

The French were both horrified and enraged. They mobilized a quick assault on the Natchez nation with orders to remove the tribe from the very face of the Earth.

The Natchez Indians were hunted down and slaughtered – no mercy was shown.

Many of the Natchez people were killed with the same fervor of the Rosalie massacre. Others were captured and tortured – some were returned to New Orleans and publicly burned at the stake. All in all, thousands were killed, and those that were spared were sold into slavery.

The few Natchez Indians that did escape sought refuge with other tribes that opposed the French, and were assimilated into their way of life. The Natchez, the once honorable and prosperous people, had been driven into extinction.

France maintained a small military garrison at a rebuilt Fort Rosalie until 1763, when the English took control of the Natchez area under the terms of the Treaty of Paris. Today, the only reminder of Fort Rosalie is a marker to commemorate where the fortress once stood on the grand cliffs overlooking the Mississippi River.

The Site of Fort Rosalee Today

The British, The Spanish, and the Americans

In 1756 a war started in Europe that would eventually change Natchez' history forever. It ended in 1763, seven years later, and was therefore dubbed the Seven Years' War. The conflict would come to involve all major European powers of the day, and the death toll neared 1.5 million. It distilled down to Great Britain and its colonies fighting Austria, France, Russia, Sweden and Spain. Winston Churchill described it as the first "world war."

Great Britain emerged victorious, taking over many of the territories of the opposing countries. The resulting Treaty of Paris, also called the Treaty of 1763, was signed on February 10th, 1763 by the kingdoms of Great Britain, France and Spain. In the agreement, France was stripped of its possessions in North America, including that of the Natchez Territory.

British soldiers occupied the area and immediately began

to put their mark there. Not only did they rename Fort Rosalie as Fort Panmure, but they also encouraged the settlers arriving with them to move into the areas surrounding the fort. These people brought with them their Protestant faith – England wanted to firmly plant its spiritual culture there.

The British basically viewed Fort Panmure as an outpost to protect their northern settlements. Soldiers of the British Empire utilized the site more as a military station than as a means for colonization, so the area never grew as an organized city, even though England held the Fort and surrounding lands for about fifteen years.

The American Revolution began in 1775, which greatly distracted Britain. Interestingly enough, for a very short time in 1778 American forces held the Natchez area. In that year, a man named James Willing took an expedition down the Mississippi River; this was supported by the United States government, which was still embroiled in its fight for independence from England. He was accompanied by a militia of about thirty men, all on the armed riverboat *Rattletrap*.

They captured the settlement around Fort Panmure on the afternoon of Friday, February 19th, and a notice was sent that all citizens should gather to be taken as prisoners of war. Since their only protection, Fort Panmure, had already fallen, the people were left with no choice. They negotiated an agreement by which they and their families would be left unharmed, but they would take an oath not to raise arms against the United States.

Willing and many of the men continued down the Mississippi. They hit strategic military targets, such as the British gunship *Rebecca*, but they also raided civilian plantations – Willing's notoriety grew and his antics were eventually deemed a "crusade of confiscation and cruelty." He and his men continued on, and although he tried to convince settlers to join the cause of the Americans, the pillaging by Willing and his men made the people doubt the integrity of the

15

new government.

When he reached New Orleans Willing sold the *Rattletrap*, and spent all the money that they had collected on "riotous living and debauchery." The citizenry of the region soon turned on Willing and he fled back east to Philadelphia, where he was captured by the British. The Willing Expedition, as it came to be known, was a total and complete disaster.

Spain began to slowly send troops and settlers farther north into Louisiana and Mississippi, and in 1778 the power shifted again – the Spanish were in control, and Manuel Gayoso de Lemos was named as the first governor of the Natchez District. He envisioned a proper city there that would reflect the stately culture of Spain. He also was convinced that the growth of the district needed a civilized infrastructure, which would be provided by establishing such a city.

The transition from the English to the Spanish wasn't without its problems – there was a bit of trouble that briefly arose in 1781, when the British citizens living in the Natchez District laid siege to Fort Panmure, but it was retaken by the Spanish; the leaders of the rebellion were tried, but released to promote the good will of the new government. Although it had been quickly dealt with, this small uprising was known as the Natchez Rebellion of 1781.

Gayoso became even more intent on seeing a formal city established, so he had the boundaries of the new city surveyed. It consisted of thirty-four city blocks surrounding a central plaza, along with a Catholic church in the center of town. All of this was adjacent to the fort, and the survey was completed in 1790. The city of Natchez prospered under Gayoso. By 1795, however, the Spanish saw the handwriting on the wall... the U.S. was coming.

The U.S. was opening its diplomatic relations with the governments around the world, and it was taking notice of foreign powers with a hold on the North American continent.

Spain opened a dialogue with the U.S. regarding that topic, and it resulted in the Treaty of San Lorenzo of 1795. In that treaty, Spain relinquished all claims to the Natchez District and its lands along the Mississippi River. It took some time for the transition to happen, and it is quite an interesting story. You'll find out more about that later in the chapter on *The House On Ellicott's Hill...*

The Natchez Trace

If you're ready for a road trip look no further than the beautiful Natchez Trace. It started as an animal trail through the wilderness, but in today's world, the Natchez Trace is a paved road that links Natchez, Mississippi with Nashville, Tennessee. It is a 444-mile scenic parkway whose beauty and serenity will delight most any traveler. The Natchez Trace has its roots far back in history, though – in fact, some aspects of its beginning may never be known.

Scientists have conflicting facts as to when the Trace originated, but some research indicates that large animals such as bison, giant sloths, deer and wolves first wore down the path over 10,000 years ago, long before humans would have been using the trail. There was a natural migration that might have established the path as animals traveled north to the salt licks in the Nashville area.

As the mound-building Natchez Indians came onto the scene, they took advantage of the natural trail, and made the lower part of the trace into more of an established roadway. Other tribes such as the Choctaw and Chickasaw may have also used the Trace for trade routes, because each Nation controlled their own portion of the Trace. In fact, as more people began to use it, different parts of the trail were given names relating to those tribes. Northeast of the Natchez Region it was called the "Path to the Choctaw Nation." The middle part of the Traces was called the "Choctaw-Chickasaw Trail," and the northern part was the "Chickasaw Trace."

It had other monikers throughout the years: "Mountain Leader's Trace," "the Natchez Road," "the Federal Road," the "Boatman's Trail," and after the city had been established, the "Natchez Trace."

Traffic along the Trace increased during the late 1700s, when travel between New Orleans and the Eastern states escalated. In 1801, the U.S. Government began using the Trace as a postal route. President Thomas Jefferson ordered the army to clear the road for the postal service, so underbrush along the way was cleared and bridges were built. In 1806, Congress voted to provide $6,000 to the U.S. Postmaster General to hire independent contractors to continue the improvements, and within a few years the Trace had became an important frontier road. When the mail route had been completed, it was officially named, "Road from Nashville in the State of Tennessee to the Grindstone Ford of the Bayou Pierre in the Mississippi Territory" – talk about a mouthful! To ensure safety for the letter carriers, treaties were negotiated with neighboring tribes such as the Chickasaw and the Choctaw. Part of the text of the 1801 Chickasaw treat reads:

"The Mingco, principal men and warriors of the Chickasaw nation of Indians, give leave and permission to the President of the United States of America, to lay out, open and make a convenient wagon road through their land between the

settlements of Mero District in the state of Tennessee, and those of Natchez in the Mississippi Territory, in such way and manner as he may deem proper; and the same shall be a high way for the citizens of the United States, and the Chickasaws. "

During the early 1800s, the Natchez Trace could be traveled by wagon from one end to the other, and was used by "flatboaters" returning home from selling their goods. These enterprising men from as far north as Illinois and as far east as Kentucky would build rectangular flat wooden boats to transport whatever products they had to carry to market. They would then use the network of rivers to reach ports such as Natchez and New Orleans. Once at their destination, the flatboats were no longer of any use, since they couldn't navigate back upriver against the current. The boats would be disassembled and sold for lumber, and the men would start their journey home on foot or by horseback – they found the Natchez Trace to be very useful for passage back home. Trading posts and inns began to spring up to service these travelers, because it took about twenty days to completely traverse the Trace.

As travel along the waterways became more popular, the Trace became less used and fewer people were found wandering along the trail. It then became a haven for robbers and villains – this was the period during which the Natchez Trace gained its notoriety. There were terrible stories about the fate that befell travelers; the most popular tale that was spread was that innocent people were routinely killed for the money that they were carrying. They were then disemboweled and their insides stuffed with rocks, and the bodies were submerged in the streams and rivers along the way. By 1830, it had been abandoned by most civilized travelers.

Almost a hundred years later, a revival of the Trace brought it to the attention of the nation once again. Construction on an automobile-navigable road along the trace was started in 1937, and it was adopted by the National Park

Service a year later.

Today, the 444-mile roadway is beautiful, easy driving, and a traveler can find many interesting places to investigate, including many that are near Natchez.

The Old Trace

There are several places along the way that you can view the old Trace as it looked in the pioneer days, and one of them is just a few miles from Natchez at marker 8.7.

A Section of the Old Trace

The text of the sign marking the Old Trace reads:

"Across the Parkway behind you is a portion of the Old Natchez Trace – a wilderness road that originated from a series of trails used by the southeastern Indian tribes. The Natchez Trace was politically, economically, socially, and militarily important for the United States in its early

22

development. *Among those that traveled this road were American Indians, traders, soldiers, "Kaintucks," postriders, settlers, slaves, circuit-riding preachers, outlaws, and adventurers. The Old Natchez Trace serves as a reminder of those who contributed to events that shaped the broad patterns of our common history.*
– National Park Service"

Emerald Mound
The mound-building Indians that left their mark on the countryside, and one of the largest mounds in North America is located at mile marker 10.3 of the Natchez Trace. It is huge – eight acres – and rises thirty-five feet high. Two smaller mounds crown the gigantic, earthen structure. Emerald Mound was first constructed by ancestors of the Natchez Indians sometime between 1250 and 1600 A.D.

Emerald Mound

23

The text of the sign marking Emerald Mound reads:
"Before you is the second largest temple mound in the United States. Only Monks Mound in Cahokia, Illinois, is larger. This eight acre mound, constructed from a natural hill, was built and used from about 1300 to 1600 by the Mississippians, ancestors of the Natchez Indians.

Unlike dome shaped mounds constructed only for burials, Emerald Mound supported temples, ceremonial structures, and burials of a complex society's civic and religious leaders.

– National Park Service"

Loess Bluff

The famous Natchez bluffs that you hear so much about are actually made of a type of soil known as "loess," which is not just your garden-variety dirt. Loess particles are very uniform, spherical particles that are 0.002mm to 0.05mm in size. Water drains from loess soil quite well because of the uniform spaces between the particles. To keep this from getting too boring, think of loess soil like a large metal drum filled with baseballs. If one were to drill holes in the bottom of the drum and pour water into the top, the water would easily drain from it. Other soil types such as clay contain size particles of infinitely different sizes, and the smaller ones clog up the spaces between the larger ones, making the soil very dense.

The problem occurs when the loess soil becomes completely saturated with water. The particles stop adhering to each other, and in the example above it would be as if you plugged the bottom holes and suddenly removed the metal drum – the baseballs would wash quickly away.

You will find loess bluffs in Natchez along the Mississippi River that the Army Corps of Engineers has reinforced to protect their integrity. Bluffs of this type are also visible out on the golf course at Beau Pre' Country Club, and many other places throughout the region.

You'll see loess bluffs all around the area, but a very good

24

example of loess bluffs is visible at mile marker 12.4 of the Natchez Trace.

A Typical Loess Bluff

The text of the sign marking this Loess Bluff reads:

"This bluff shows a deep deposit of windblown topsoil known as loess (pronounced LOW-ess). It was formed during the Ice Age when glaciers covered the northern half of the United States. At this time nearly continuous dust storms swept in from the western plains and covered this area with windblown dust to a depth of 30 to 90 feet. Here it rests on sands and clays of an ancient sea. It originally covered a vast region but in this area is now confined to a strip east of the Mississippi River from 3 to 30 miles wide extending from Baton Rouge into Tennessee. Where the old Natchez Traced passed over loess it formed sunken roads, in places 20 feet deep.

– National Park Service"

Mount Locust

Located at mile 15.5 of the Trace is Mount Locust, one of Mississippi's oldest structures. Built in the 1780s, it was a plantation and an inn for weary travelers. This structure is the only one of the fifty-plus inns that once dotted the Natchez Trace during its heyday.

It has been restored to include several of the rooms as they might have looked when the house was in use – it's well worth a stop.

The Steps Leading Up To Mount Locust

The text of the sign marking Mount Locust reads:

"Constructed circa 1780, this home is one of the oldest structures in Mississippi. It functioned as both a working plantation and as an inn, where travelers on the Natchez Trace could rest for the night. Mount Locust is the only surviving inn of more than 50 that existed during the period of greatest use

of the Old Natchez Trace.
– Mississippi State Society, D.A.R. "

The Public Room of Mount Locust

These are just a few of the places on the Natchez Trace worth visiting – it is a place brimming with history, archeology and natural beauty.

A Great Steak and a Ghost Named Madeline

The first thing that you will notice when you enter King's Tavern is that the door is perhaps a little more narrow then most doors, and it's quite heavy; you have to use a little extra force to swing it open.

As you step into the restaurant, be sure to look down – you'll see a well-worn wooden step that has been there for as long as anyone can imagine. As you put your foot on it to enter, just pause a moment and reflect on those who tread there before you: early settlers of Natchez, dignitaries from around the world, river pirates from the wild days of the Mississippi, and of course, outlaws who preyed on travelers making their way down the Natchez Trace. It is literally impossible to envision all the visitors to the Tavern, because people have been stepping through that doorway since it was built sometime around 1789.

Records indicate that a land grant was posted on May 31, 1789, deeding the land to Mr. Prosper King, the restaurant's namesake. It is assumed that he constructed the building as a tavern and inn. Travelers up and down the Trace would stop for a rest, a meal, or a room for the night. Locals would stop in for a tankard of ale and to pick up their mail, which was dropped off at the tavern by passing postal carriers. Outlaws would gather in the tavern because there was safety in numbers – it was one thing to hide in the shadows of the Trace, but in public there was always the threat of lawmen, vigilante groups, or anyone with a grudge or vengeance.

One of the most notorious stories from King's Tavern concerns a very nasty outlaw named Big Harpe – you'll read more about him and his brother in the "Outlaws of the Trace" chapter of this book. As the legend goes, Big Harpe had been enjoying a healthy portion of ale at the Tavern with his cronies one evening. Their party atmosphere had been continually interrupted by an infant whose constant crying resounded through the building. The mother took the child to the small mailroom to try and comfort her, which is when Big Harpe decided to lend his assistance… and he did the unthinkable. He walked into the mailroom, took the infant from the mother's arms, grabbed her feet and ankles in his massive hand, then swung the child like a baseball bat, bashing her head against the wall. He put the lifeless baby back in her mother's arms as if she were a rag doll, then went back to his friends to carry on with the party.

Another legend about the tavern is about the owner, Prosper King himself. Even though he was a married man, supposedly he had a mistress named Madeline. Whether they would rendezvous in the upper rooms of the tavern that were usually rented out to travelers, or whether they met at more discreet places in Natchez, no one will ever know for sure. In

29

fact, the conclusion to this story is pure Natchez legend.

As the story goes, Mrs. King found out about the illicit affair. She didn't dare punish her husband, a successful Natchez businessman and owner of the inn and tavern, so she did the next best thing – she hired men to take Madeline's life.

The Main Dining Room of King's Tavern

That's where the legend ends, but not the story itself. In the early 1900s, a chimney collapsed in the tavern, and a jeweled, Spanish dagger was found in the rubble. There were many questions as to why it was there, and what it had been used for. A few decades later when renovations were being done on the building, three skeletons were found behind the fireplace, entombed in the ground floor wall – two men, and one woman. The woman has always been assumed to be Madeline, but the identity of the men remains a mystery. If Mrs. King did have Madeline killed, did she somehow do in the assassins to keep her secret? No one will even know for sure, but these poor individuals, whoever they are, will forever be part of King's Tavern lore.

In today's world, a host or hostess will greet you and start you on an incredible culinary journey into the restaurant. You will dine beneath the low ceiling with its exposed beams, the legendary fireplace just paces away. King's Tavern boasts an impressive wine list, and a menu that will tantalize your taste buds.

The Tavern, And The Flags That Have Flown Over Natchez

As always, along with the incredible food, visitors enjoy talking to the waitstaff about the hauntings at King's Tavern. Guests always want to climb the stairs to the upper floors in hopes of seeing a ghost, but that rarely happens. The tavern is most active when things are still and quiet.

On the third floor, in the bedroom, local legend says that if

31

you pass your hand an inch or so over the bedspread you can feel the warmth of the lady who still comes back to sleep there long after her death.

The Third Floor Bedroom

A baby's cry can be heard in the first floor of the restaurant, even though the front doors are locked securely. One waitress that I spoke to said that more that once members of the staff had heard the cries, and went to see who'd brought an infant in before the tavern was open. This phenomenon is always attributed to the baby who allegedly became the victim of the outlaw Big Harpe.

A woman has also been seen standing in the restaurant, especially near the fireplace, often mistaken for a customer, even thought the restaurant was closed. She vanishes as quickly as she appears, so the employees simply assume that Madeline has come back for a visit.

There are many more supernatural occurrences at King's Tavern, including wine glasses and bottles that move on their own, and little mischievous occurrences that keep the staff on their toes.

While you may not experience the touch of the paranormal at the restaurant, you will definitely enjoy some incredible food. As much as people love the ghost stories of King's Tavern, they love the food even more.

King's Tavern
619 Jefferson Street
Natchez, MS 39120-3319
601.446.8845

Linden

Although you can tour the spectacular "Linden" during the Spring or Fall Pilgrimage in Natchez, the best way to experience the old mansion is to stay there for the evening. Most rooms open up to the back gallery where you will find antique rocking chairs that will allow you to sit and contemplate the peaceful days of long ago. It is a wonderful place to unwind with a book or a glass of wine, and while you're there, you will truly learn the meaning of the word "relaxation."

The beautiful house known as Linden originally started as a property that was a Spanish land grant of 150 acres made to Madam Sarah Truly back in 1785, well over two hundred years ago. Sarah Truly held the property for a few years, before finally selling it to Alexander Moore, a prominent Natchez merchant.

It wasn't Alexander who started construction, though, but instead his son James who built the original part of the house in 1792. It was a cottage with two rooms downstairs separated by a hallway, and the same configuration on the second floor.

In 1818, Linden was purchased by Senator Thomas Reed, who was the first elected senator for the newly admitted State of Mississippi. He added the hand-carved wooden columns to the doorway, along with other adornments including the sidelights and fanlight. It is said that Linden's doorway was so beautiful that it was copied for a home in the film *Gone With the Wind*. In addition to that, Thomas Reed built the East wing to the house that included four new bedrooms. At that time, the house was named "Reedland" in honor of its owner.

In 1829 a new owner acquired the property – "Reedland" was purchased by Doctor John Ker, who added the dining room to the house. Little by little, it grew into the beautiful home that it is today. Ker didn't much care for the house's moniker, though, so he changed the name of the property to "Linden." Since his family was of German descent, and the Linden tree was the national tree of Germany, this seemed like a natural choice.

Some twenty years later, Linden was sold to a widow, Mrs. Jane Gustine Conner. Like every previous owner, she added to the house – this time it was the West wing, which contained the warming kitchens and keeping rooms downstairs, and the schoolroom upstairs. She also built an outbuilding that was a bowling alley for her children's amusement. The schoolroom was a necessity, since she had thirteen children to educate. Her husband had just died, and she was looking for a place in town that would be appropriate to raise her children.

After the Civil War broke out, Mrs. Conner became known as "The Little War Mother" because she had eight sons serving the Confederacy, along with five sons-in-law. Every male was off fighting for the Southern cause, leaving the women there alone.

One of Mrs. Conner's daughters who was married to General Martin of the Confederate army abandoned her home "Montaigne" during the war, and moved a majority of her possessions to Linden. She stored them not only in the main house but also the outlying buildings, including the bowling alley.

During the Northern Army's occupation of Natchez, Mrs. Conner was in her kitchen one day, only to look out and see the Union soldiers removing her daughter's things from the bowling alley building. Without hesitation, she marched outside and stooped down to pick up a handful of rocks along the way.

She confronted the soldiers and informed them that while she couldn't prevent them from stealing her daughter's furniture, she could certainly keep them from enjoying the mirrors that adorned several of the items. She dug into her apron pockets, producing several of the stones that she'd picked up, and drew her arm back to carry out her threat. The soldiers stopped her, and returned the furniture back to the bowling alley building. They had probably never before encountered a woman such as Mrs. Conner.

Today, Linden is a beautiful example of a Federal style home; it is furnished in mostly Federal style furniture, but also includes Chippendale and early Empire furnishings. It is a showplace of the Old South.

The house is now owned by Jeanette Feltus, and her daughters are the sixth generation of the Conner family to have occupied Linden. Along with the history of the house, she also has a few ghost stories to tell about the old place – a phantom buggy that rides in front of the house, a spectral lady that was seen walking on the top of the East wing, and even a man in a top hat that appeared in the house. Not to worry, though… these are all just shadows of Linden's past, and nothing to be frightened of. In fact, it seems that some of the former owners of the house are simply looking back in from time to time. For

36

example, a man is heard walking along the rear gallery; specifically, the tapping of a cane is heard. Not only has Mrs. Feltus experienced this, but she has had B&B guests come down to breakfast and question who was walking up and down the gallery the previous evening.

Should you decide to spend some time there, Linden has six guestrooms, each with a private bath. All bedrooms are furnished with canopied beds and antiques. Most of the bedrooms open onto the back gallery, where you will find antique rocking chairs for your pleasure and relaxation. Guests can also enjoy a plantation breakfast that is served in the dining room every morning. It is truly an experience that you will always remember.

Linden Bed and Breakfast
1 Linden Place
Natchez, MS 39120
601.445.5472
www.lindenbandb.com

The House on Ellicott Hill

Natchez had no idea what it was getting when President George Washington dispatched a rather rotund Quaker from Pennsylvania to town in 1796. His name was Major Andrew Ellicott, and he was sent there as an American commissioner to settle the boundary dispute that the new country was having with Spain over the borders negotiated in the Treaty of San Lorenzo. Ellicott was a man extremely qualified for the job – he had made the first official measurements of Niagara Falls, and had been appointed to the position as the country's Surveyor-General. Other aspects of his personality may have made him even more appropriate for the task, however; even though he was a Quaker, there is nothing in the world that the Major enjoyed more than a good, old-fashioned fist fight. He was well known, in fact, for his roughhousing ways.

On his arrival in town in 1797, Ellicott contacted the

Governor of the Natchez district, Manuel Luis Gayoso de Lemos, to present his credentials and establish the parameters for the surveying mission. Governor Gayoso managed to delay their meeting time and time again, until it became obvious that the governor was stalling for some reason. Ellicott's temper began to rise, until he finally confronted Gayoso and demanded that he be allowed to start the survey. An accord was reached and plans were made.

Ellicott soon learned that there was an undercurrent of deception, however, and that Gayoso planned on continuing to inject delays to the survey. The large Quaker had reached his boiling point; he chose a hill overlooking the city, established a camp there, and planted an American flag as if to claim the hill for the United States.

Ellicott's bold actions did not go unnoticed. There was an uproar among the Spanish, and Governor Gayoso sent a letter demanding that the flag be removed. Ellicott refused, strutting defiantly around the city, and starting a slow, steady campaign for American rule in Natchez. Ellicott soon took up residence in Connelly's Tavern, about a block from where he had established his famous camp. He would stay in Natchez for the next few years, before returning to Pennsylvania to settle down with his family. It is interesting to note that several years later, President Thomas Jefferson asked Ellicott to serve as a mentor for a Mr. Meriwether Lewis, who was going to team with William Clark for an expedition across America. Lewis lived at Ellicott's Pennsylvania home for several months where Ellicott gave his opinions and instruction on both equipment and survey procedures for the Lewis and Clark expedition.

Meanwhile, back in Natchez, a well-to-do merchant named James Moore obtained the plot of land that Ellicott had been using for his camp – during the Spanish rule, only wealthy men were allowed to purchase land on Canal Street, since it was the most prominent section of town. Moore constructed his home there overlooking the Mississippi River.

The winds of change were soon blowing across Natchez again – in 1795 the Pinckney Treaty was signed between Spain and the United States. It finally settled the land dispute, and called for Spain to pull out from the Natchez District and surrender it to the U.S.

On March 30, 1798, the last Spanish soldier withdrew from the city, and Major Isaac Guion officially raised the American flag – reportedly on the hill where Ellicott had planted his a year before. James Moore continued to live in the house there until he married in 1799.

Ralph Waldo Emerson once said, "A man's wife has more power over him than the state has." That may have certainly been true in Moore's marriage, because his wife insisted that they live not at the House on Ellicott Hill, but instead at their plantation house located on the Liberty Road. The groom acquiesced, and the house on the hill was turned into rental property for the family.

The first renter was Samuel Brooks; under the American rule, he became the first mayor of the city of Natchez in 1803. The Brooks family lived in the house until 1807, when Dr. Frederic Seip took residence there. A prominent physician, he was appointed to the post of Health Officer for the city of Natchez in 1818. The doctor enjoyed a dozen good years on the hill, until he passed away. His wife and son continued to rent the house until 1825, and at that point, James Moore sold the house that he had built on Ellicott's Hill.

The house still didn't have a permanent resident; a real-estate speculator named Orlando Lane purchased the home and land and kept it as rental property. Not only were there several tenants over the course of that period who used it strictly for living quarters, but for a time it was even operated as a coffeehouse.

The rear of the house, from the entry on top of the hill

The house had a major change in 1850, however, when the property was purchased by a group that established the *Natchez High School for Boys* there. It was an exclusive, private boarding school for the young men of the town from affluent families, serving Natchez for twenty-eight years.

When the school finally closed, the house on the hill was relegated to simply being housing for workers at the local cotton mills, and as one might imagine, it began to fall into disrepair. When the mills closed in the 1920s, the majestic House on Ellicott Hill was abandoned, and it would remain in that state until 1934.

At that time the beautiful, old property was rescued by the Natchez Garden Club. With vision of preserving the historic

41

home, they conducted the first restoration of such a property by a civic organization in the entire state of Mississippi. Today, the house is open to the public for tours; it is beautifully furnished, based on the original inventories from the Moore and Seip families on the site where Andrew Ellicott first planted the American flag. Today, the flag of 1797 is still flown on Ellicott's Hill, commemorating the day when he took that stand for the United States of America.

The House On Ellicott Hill
211 North Canal St.
Natchez, MS
601.442.2011
www.natchezgardenclub.com

The Town of Rodney

If you're up for a driving adventure, just try finding the town of Rodney, located a little south of Alcorn University. It is a ghost town, really, since its majesty is long gone and few people live there today.

The town of Rodney, originally known as Petit Gulf, was founded in 1798. Maps exist that show the name all the way back to 1715, and historians believe that this spot was used by Native Americans to cross the Mississippi, which during that period ran beside the city. The town's name was changed in 1814 to honor Judge Thomas Rodney, the territorial magistrate.

When Mississippi was seeking statehood in the early 1800s, Rodney missed becoming the capitol of the Mississippi Territory by only 3 votes. In the 1850s, it was quite the bustling place – after all, it had the state's first opera house, 1000 permanent residents, a huge hotel with a ballroom, 35 stores,

43

and two banks. At the time, Rodney was considered to be the busiest riverport on the Mississippi between New Orleans and St. Louis. Steamships such as the *Robert E. Lee* and the *Natchez* regularly stopped at the city.

By 1860 the town had over four thousand residents who were served by several newspapers: *The Rodney Gazette, The Southern Telegraph, The Rodney Standard* and *The Rodney Telegraph.*

During its heyday, Rodney played host to many notable visitors, including Andrew Jackson, congressman and Secretary of State Henry Clay, and twelfth President of the United States Zachary Taylor. Taylor was so taken by the countryside that he purchased Cypress Grove Plantation.

Rodney is best known for an incident that took place there during the Civil War. Once Vicksburg had fallen, the Union Navy kept a close watch on the Mississippi River. The gunboat *Rattler* had positioned itself beside the port of Rodney to contain any Confederate activity. Every Sunday morning, it is said that the men on board would line the deck of the ship to watch the southern belles as they walked down the streets in their finest dresses to attend church.

Although the crew was under strict orders not to leave the ship, on September 13, 1863, nineteen (the actual number varies depending on the source of the story, up to twenty-four) of the Union officers and mates disembarked to attend church services with the lovely ladies that they had been watching. They filed into the Presbyterian Church, attired in their dress uniforms, and took their place in the congregation. During the second hymn of worship, Lieutenant Allen of the Confederate Cavalry strode up the aisle and took the pulpit. He apologized to the pastor, Reverend Baker, announcing that his men had surrounded the church. Panic swept through the people, and one Yankee sailor took refuge behind a door and shot at the Lieutenant. The civilians fled in a panic, and one sailor even hid under the skirt of a local girl that he'd befriended. An

44

elderly lady remained calm, though, and even stood up on a pew and shouted, "Glory to God!"

The crew of the *Rattler* knew that their companions were in danger, and turned their large guns on the town, hitting several homes and the church itself.

The interior of the church

Confederate Lieutenant Allen quickly sent word to the gunboat that, "the people of Rodney were in no way responsible for what my men have done, and if another solitary shell is thrown into the town, I will proceed to hang my prisoners."

It was the first time in the history of warfare that a cavalry troop had captured the crew of a naval gunboat, and the *Rattler* and its crew became a joke on both sides of the war; the Rebel soldiers had made the capture without firing a shot.

Local legend adds a tender note to this story, however. The

45

Yankee soldier that hid under the skirt of the lady reportedly escaped from capture by the Confederates, and after the war, he returned to Rodney with the intent of marrying her to show his appreciation for her life-saving courage. As was often the case in those days, though, disease had taken her life, and the gentleman returned north heartbroken and empty-handed.

The balcony in back of the church, used by the slaves during worship; note the ladder and bell tower access

In 1870 the Mississippi River started changing course, and unfortunately the result left the town of Rodney high and dry. By 1940 it was three miles inland, and most people had moved away.

Some people still live there, preserving its legends and history. Several historical markers surround the church, and here are a few of the more interesting ones that tell the story of the town of Rodney:

HISTORY OF RODNEY – HER RISE

The French were the first Europeans to claim this area, called "Petit Gouffre," "Petit Golphe," "Petit Gulf," or "Little Gulf". In 1763, as a result of the French and Indian War, the area became the dominion of Great Britain. Spain captured British West Florida in 1781, and controlled this area until 1798. A 1791 Spanish land grant deeded the site of present-day Rodney to Thomas Calvit, a prominent territorial Mississippi landholder. Rodney was incorporated in 1828 and named in honor of Thomas Rodney, territorial judge who presided at the Aaron Burr hearing. Rodney area citizens gave much support to Oakland College. The college influenced the entire rural area, and Rodney was a community of an unusually high level of culture. General Zachery Taylor owned Cypress Grove Plantation, a few miles south of town, and was a frequent visitor to Rodney. It is said he was there when elected President of the United States. As river transportation improved, Rodney grew in population and in size, and became a flourishing river town. In the early 1830s, the population was about 200, and there were 20 stores, a church, a bank, and a newspaper. In the late 1850s, Rodney was noted for its county fairs, and was visited by people from all over the Mississippi Valley.

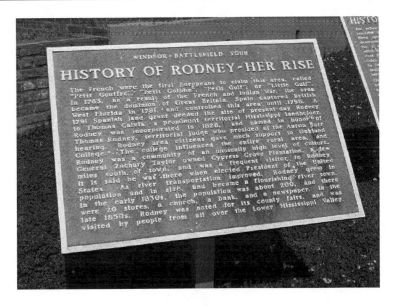

OLD RODNEY PRESBYTERIAN CHURCH

Listed in the National Register of Historic Places, the church was begun when the 1828 Mississippi Legislature granted a charter of incorporation to the "Presbyterian Church of Petit Gulf". Later in 1828, the Town of Rodney was incorporated, the community and church becoming known as Rodney rather than Petit Gulf. Presbyterian activity in Rodney was apparent prior to erection of the present church structure in 1830-31. When Rev. John Hutchinson came in 1830 as supply minister for one year, there were at least two members and services were held in a barroom. The present brick church was dedicated to the worship of God on the first day of 1832. The dedication sermon was preached by Rev. Dr. Jeremiah Chamberlain, founder and president of Oakland College. According to tradition, one thousand silver dollars were cast into the mold of the church bell. The cemetery is located on the wooded bluff east of the church, and contains remains of Civil War trenches and graves of river travelers.

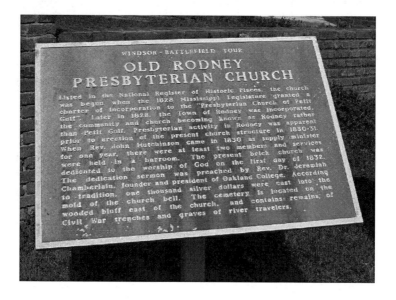

OLD TOWN OF RODNEY – LAYOUT

The earliest references to the Rodney area are from the 1774 New England expedition led by General Phineas Lyman to organize a settlement on Big Black River. Captain Matthew Phelps, a member of this expedition, described the area as "Firm rock on the est side of the Mississippi for near a mile. The land near the river is high, very broken, very rich, and several plantations have been opened." A sketch of Rodney in 1828 by French naturalist and painter Charles Lesueur revealed about 20 buildings leading from the river to the prominent bluff behind town. Two structures were two-story; others were one-story. An 1853 map indicates that Church, Cypress, Magnolia, and Spring Streets lay east and west, and that Commerce and Olive Streets lay north and south. As the town grew, new streets were added; Batchelor and Griffing lay east and west, while St. Peter's lay north and south between these two. These streets, excepting Commerce which has been paved, are now merely dirt roads or have disappeared entirely. Prior to new road construction of the 1960's, the only accessible routes to Rodney were several "sunken" dirt, but very scenic, roads lined by moss-draped, vine-covered trees.

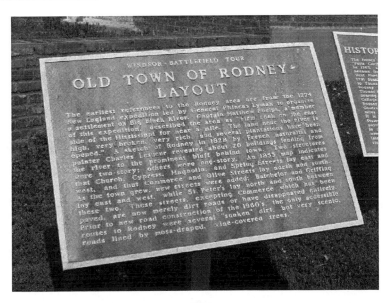

49

HISTORY OF RODNEY – HER FALL

The yellow fever epidemics of 1843 and 1898 were fatal to many residents of Rodney. Even though the Union gunboat "Rattler" fired upon the town, Rodney and her churches were spared destruction during the Civil War. Here was the disembarking point for a select detachment of 40 Union Calvary (Fifth Illinois), which launched a raid to the east behind Confederate lines in June 1863. The Confederates won this engagement, capturing the Union troops which sought to raid the Mobile and Ohio Railroad. In September 1864, Union troops were sent from Vicksburg to destroy a reported Confederate troop concentration at Rodney. Landing here, the Union Infantry regiment plundered almost every house in town. Citizens of Rodney area formed Company D, 22nd Mississippi Infantry, which fought for the Confederacy. At war's end, a sand bar formed in the Mississippi River, causing the River to alter its course, moving two miles west of Rodney. Tragedy struck in 1869 when a fire almost completely destroyed the town. The population further declined after the 1880's when a railroad was constructed to the east through Fayette. By executive proclamation, Governor Bilbo in 1930 abolished this century-old town of Rodney.

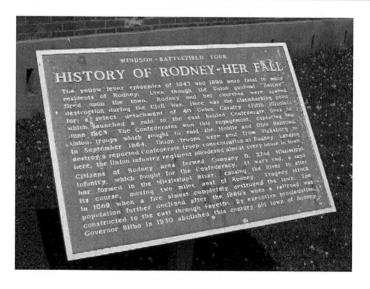

Unless you know exactly how to get there, Rodney can be incredibly hard to find. It is easy to drive down every back road between Alcorn University and Natchez and still not run across it.

If you have directions, though, it's actually quite an easy drive that takes under an hour from Natchez.

Directions to Rodney:
- From Natchez, go north on the Trace to the 30 mile marker
- Take the next exit – Hwy 552/Alcorn State University
- Take 552 west toward the Windsor Ruins – go 2 miles
- Take a left on Fellowship Road – go .5 miles
- Take a left at the large, white Lorman Waterworks water tank – go 1 mile
- Take a right at the stop sign – go 6 miles to Rodney
- When the road dead-ends, the church is just down the street on the right.

The Hanging Tree
of Old Natchez

In the center of the historic district you'll find the stately Adams County Courthouse. It was built in 1821, but even before that time the land that it is built on was used as a public meeting place.

In 1799 it was an open market where people peddled their crops and other wares. The block was also used for public meetings and events, including auctions and political rallies. Legend has it that Andrew Jackson once stood on a box in the square and made an impassioned speech to the men of the city, recruiting them to fight in the War of 1812.

The square was also used to hold court, and when a suspect was found guilty of a crime punishable by death, the tree on the southwest corner was used to dispatch justice quickly. It became known as the "hanging tree," a moniker that it holds to this day.

After the courthouse was built in 1821, the tree's terrible purpose continued. According to Robert and Jacqueline Stephens, local historians and former proprietors of the Natchez Ghost Walk, there are quite a few documented hangings at the tree – as many as three hundred. Those for which the documentation has been lost to history probably push the actual number much higher. If you examine the records, the crimes are mostly for horse thievery, murder and other serious crimes of the day. In some cases, the crimes didn't seem as serious; people convicted of petty theft were even hanged at the tree, so in such cases it must have been chronic, repeat criminals.

Justice was swift in those days. The condemned man was made to stand on a chair or stool and the rope was placed around his neck. The executioner would then kick the chair from under his legs and the prisoner would fall. In the most merciful cases his neck would snap immediately. On some occasions however, his noose would tighten in the fall and the victim would flail about, even though his hands and legs were bound. In that instance, it is said that a relative, even the wife of the condemned, would break free from the crowd and grab their loved one's legs, pulling them down with all their weight to end the suffering. During the Natchez Ghost Walk, Robert pointed out that this was the origin of the term, "pulling your leg."

The hangings at the tree continued until 1891, when the process of execution was formalized and moved to the new city jail just down the street. Still, the spiritual memories of the hanging tree may continue to this day. The Stephens report that many interesting, unexplainable photographs of the tree have been taken during the ghost walk. There seems to be some supernatural presence associated with the tree that persists, even though the last hanging occurred there over one hundred years ago.

During one of the Ghost Walks, while stopping at the hanging tree, one person stepped back, clutching her throat. She later said that while Stephen was talking about the hanging tree, there was a tightness at her throat, and it felt as if two cold fingers were dragging along the back of her neck – perhaps as if someone were adjusting a noose.

When the Hanging Tree became a regular stop on the ghost walk an interesting thing happened. Local residents of Natchez began to share their own experiences there. As Jacqueline explained it to me, citizens go to the courthouse for many reasons: pay taxes, renew licenses, vote, serve on jury duty, and other civic needs. Many people report that a certain spot around the tree is always colder than the outside temperature; some have shown her the exact spot. While conducting a Ghost Walk one evening, she learned that one of the people accompanying her was a psychic. When she told the group about the cold spot, the psychic walked directly to it and announced the location – even thought Jacqueline had made no indication as to where it was.

Do spirits of those who suffered a horrible death hanging from the limbs of the tree return in today's world? It seems to be entirely possible. In fact, if you visit the huge tree on the courthouse square, you may encounter some of these ghosts just hanging around (sorry, I couldn't resist).

Historic Jefferson College

What do John Wayne, George Washington and Thomas Jefferson all have in common? Well, the answer can be found a few miles northeast of Natchez on Highway 61. There a visitor will run across the town of Washington, named for the nation's first president. It's not that far, just a few miles, because Natchez is slowly expanding as the population grows. It probably won't be long before it meets the city of Washington.

Aside from serving as the capital of the Mississippi Territory from 1802 to 1817, one of the major things that Washington is known for is Jefferson College, named for another president, Thomas Jefferson. It was chartered in 1802 by the first General Assembly of the Mississippi Territory, a good fifteen years before Mississippi statehood. It was the first educational institution there and William C.C. Claiborne, the Territorial Governor, served on the first Board of Trustees.

Although the school had been recognized in 1802, it was actually another nine years before its doors were finally opened. On January 7th 1811, it was a preparatory school that welcomed fifteen students in its charter class. The school continued to grow based on donations made from private supporters and from money provided by the government. A short six years later, Jefferson had become a college. The next year, a ten-year-old boy would walk onto the campus as a student – a young man named Jefferson Davis, who would eventually become President of the Confederate States.

A Restored Classroom

New buildings were constructed to house the students; an East Wing was added in 1819, and a West Wing in 1839. In 1830 the college purchased the Methodist church building that had been used for the 1817 Mississippi statehood convention. It was literally the site where statehood began – the birthplace of the state of Mississippi.

Some of the more popular legends about Jefferson College include the fact that General Andrew Jackson camped his troops there on the way to fight the Battle of New Orleans, and that it was there Aaron Burr was tried for treason under a stand of Spanish oak trees. While evidence does point to the fact that Jackson and his troops were there, there is some question to the Aaron Burr story. Even though his hearing was held in Washington, since it was in the winter the proceedings were most likely not held outside beneath oak trees. The better explanation is that the trial was held at or around Jefferson College and the oaks were given his name to commemorate that fact. The guides there continue to get the question, "Are those oaks where Aaron Burr was put on trial?" They just shake their heads, and try to set the story straight.

The Aaron Burr Oaks

Speaking of legends, some say that the famous ornithologist John James Audubon may have taught at

Jefferson College. One of the most interesting things is that today Audubon's name is synonymous with the preservation of wildlife. To document the countless birds in North American and to do the sketches and paintings that he is famous for, he basically went hunting and shot birds that he hadn't yet included in his body of work. He would take the carcasses back to his workroom, pose them, and proceed with his drawings – something that would horrify most bird watchers today.

Whether Audubon taught at the school or not, there is a prestigious list of academic leaders associated with Jefferson College. William Dunbar, the Mississippi territory's most active man of science, was a member of the first board of directors there. Members of later Board of Directors included such notable men as Benjamin Wailes and John Wesley Monette.

In 1837, an educational and philosophical group was founded at the school named the Jefferson College and Washington Lyceum. The committees comprising the group focused on the studies of belles-lettres and mental science, moral philosophy and theology, constitutional law and political economy, natural history, mathematics and physical science, antiquities and history, and anatomy and physiology. This Lyceum published a periodic literary journal, and also undertook local archeological endeavors such as the exploration of local Natchez Indian mounds.

When the Civil War reached Mississippi in 1863, the doors to Jefferson College temporarily closed. It opened again in 1866, this time strictly as a prep school. It evolved into a military academy and the name of the school became the "Jefferson Military College." It remained as such until the doors of the school were closed again in 1964, this time for good... at least as an educational facility.

The proud campus would rise once again, because Historic Jefferson College was restored by the Mississippi Department of Archives and History in phases completed in 1977, and then again in 1984. This restoration effort was funded not only by the state, but also by the Friends of Jefferson College, a non-profit organization dedicated to the preservation of the college, and the Jefferson Military College Foundation that is composed of former students, faculty and others.

Today Jefferson College is listed on the National Register of Historic Places by the U.S. Department of the Interior, and visitors can tour many of the old buildings including a restored dormitory room, the student dining hall, the kitchen building and other historical areas. The site also features the T.J. Foster Nature Trail which winds though the nearby woods, past Ellicott Springs, named for Andrew Ellicott featured in the "House on Ellicott's Hill" chapter of this book. A visitor's center on the grounds features exhibits of recovered artifacts: dinnerware, shoes, photographs, documents, and uniforms.

Some Of The College's Supporting Buildings

It is an extremely interesting place to visit, but you may be wondering just exactly what John Wayne has to do with this historic, old school – after all, his name was mentioned at the first of this chapter. Well, when visiting Jefferson College, you may have the distinct feeling that you've been there before. Don't dismiss the sensation, though, because it may be very true. Jefferson College has been used in film and on screen many times. John Wayne's movie "The Horse Soldiers" was filmed here, as was the television mini-series "North-South," where it portrayed West Point Academy. The film "Mistress of Paradise" starring Anthony Andrews and Chad Everett filmed here as well, and two different versions of Huckleberry Finn have used the college. Chances are, you have seen this place somewhere before – on the big screen.

Historic Jefferson College
Washington, MS
601.442.2901

The Man Who Would Be King

The tales of Natchez range from the uniquely historical to the downright strange. The truth about one of the most puzzling stories associated with the city may never completely come to light, though. It is the saga of a man named Aaron Burr: Revolutionary War Hero, New York State Attorney General, United States Senator, Vice President of the U.S., and an accused traitor to the nation, who was put on trial just outside of Natchez for high treason.

Burr was born the son of a Presbyterian minister, and he was studying law when the Revolutionary War broke out. Ever the patriot, he served his country as a soldier under several different commanders, including Generals Benedict Arnold and George Washington. He distinguished himself in several battles, and became a nationally-known hero of the war, although he was never decorated with a commendation.

After the war, Burr completed his law studies, and was admitted to the bar at Albany in 1782. He began to practice law in New York City.

After serving in several public offices, he founded the Bank of the Manhattan Company, which would later become the Chase Manhattan Bank of modern times. In 1800, he aided Thomas Jefferson's campaign for presidency and was put on the ticket with him. They each received 73 electoral votes, a tie which caused the voting to go to the House of Representatives. Burr lost the ballot there by one vote – Jefferson became

61

President and Burr accepted the office of Vice President.

Jefferson felt that the political party's preference was for him to be the president; the fact that Burr almost defeated him became a bone of contention that would remain between them forever. Jefferson no longer trusted him and Burr was shut out of all political matters in the party.

During this time, Aaron Burr had a strong political rival in Alexander Hamilton – the latter's vicious comments against the former caused Burr to challenge the man to a formal duel. On July 11, 1804, the two men met outside the city of Weehawken, New Jersey and the duel commenced. Hamilton's shot missed, but Burr sent a fatal shot to his opponent, with the bullet hitting the liver and the spine. Interestingly enough, he was the first of only two Vice Presidents in American history to shoot another man while serving in office; the second incident happened many years later, in contemporary times, when Vice President Dick Chaney accidentally shot a friend while hunting.

The Duel Between Aaron Burr and Alexander Hamilton

What happened next in the life of Aaron Burr is open to debate and interpretation. It is said that when talking about his plans he never told two people the same story. In fact, he spoke in hints and innuendos, leaving people to draw their own conclusion as to his intent.

Some believe that he had purchased land in the Texas portion of Mexico, hoping to wrestle it from Spanish control for the United States. Others thought him more innocent, that he only wanted to colonize part of the Louisiana Purchase. Talk began to spread across the country that he planned to seize a large territory and declare it an independent nation, with him as its king or emperor.

He was supposedly set on raising a large sum of money for his endeavors, leading an army down along the Mississippi. Military expertise would be provided by General Wilkinson, Commander-in-Chief of the U.S. Army at New Orleans and Governor of the Louisiana Territory. When the time came for action, the grandiose plans had dwindled somewhat. Burr hadn't obtained anywhere near the sum of money that he'd hoped for, and his followers numbered under one hundred – many were families including women and children.

As the story goes, Burr set his sights on the city of Natchez, hoping to arrive there and be hailed as a hero who would set the region free from United States control. Rumors about his march were spreading across the country, and in New Orleans General Wilkinson turned against him. The General denounced Burr as a traitor to the nation and ordered his arrest. The Governor of the Mississippi Territory believed Wilkinson's words, and immediately sent soldiers out to stop this treasonous act.

Governor Mead's men met Burr and his group at Bayou Pierre. Realizing the plight that he was in, the alleged traitor decided to surrender himself and take his chances in the court system. Aaron Burr was arraigned in Natchez and was released on bond. No one could have predicted what happened next –

the people of the city welcomed him like a celebrity. Receptions were thrown in his honor, dinners were given with the best people in town attending, and everyone who was anyone wanted to brush elbows with the famous – if not downright notorious – Aaron Burr.

And then something completely unexpected happened... the controversial Mr. Burr fell in love.

A longtime friend of his had invited him to stay on his plantation, Halfway Hill. Burr received visitors there, including many ladies seeking an introduction. None of them caught his eye, though. Fate stepped in when he saw a beautiful lady walking near Halfway Hill with long brown curls and an angelic face. Madeline Price was a poor young woman living with her mother in a nearby cottage. As her father led the family to Natchez, they were attacked by a robber who took their entire life's savings, and her dad's life.

Aaron was enamored of this woman's beauty, and he made arrangements to not only meet her, but to start seeing her for dinner and at tea. The couple fell in love and Burr proposed, but Madeline informed him that he had to clear himself of the legal snares before they could take their relationship any further.

The case of treason against him was heard in the town of Washington, just out of Natchez, and as the legend goes, there were so many people in attendance that it had to be moved outdoors beneath the oak trees near Jefferson College. Whatever the crowd expected, what happened was much, much different. The Attorney General, who would be prosecuting the case against Burr, stood up and asked that the jury be dismissed due to lack of evidence against the defendant. An outcry came forth from Burr's opponents, while his supporters cried victory. The entire hearing degenerated into a disorganized mess. The judge, trying to keep order, dismissed the charges but still ordered Burr to stay in contact with the court for the foreseeable future.

The Oak Trees Under Which Burr was Rumored to be Tried

Unsure of his future, Aaron returned to Madeline and asked for her hand once again. She repeated her former answer, however: he must clear himself of all legal issues before she would consent to be his bride. Dejected, Burr got on his horse and road away... only to be captured by the authorities a few miles away, who surmised that he was fleeing the judge's orders.

Burr was tried once again, and he was again acquitted of any charges. This time he knew that his career in America was over, so he fled to Europe to salvage whatever part of his life that he could and to escape his many creditors. Madeline was left alone in Natchez.

Finally, over a year later, she received a letter from Aaron Burr. It said that they would never be together and that Madeline should enter a convent and become a nun.

Burr lived in England for some time, but when he started up his political plans once again, he was ordered out of the country. He wanted to move to France but Napoleon Bonaparte refused to receive him. With nowhere else to go, he returned to America and adopted the name "Edwards," his mother's maiden name, so that he could avoid creditors.

Aaron Burr suffered a debilitating stroke in 1834, and was left completely immobile. He died two years later on Staten Island.

And Madeline? She did not heed his advice to join a convent and become a nun. Instead, she vacationed in Havana, and met an English man who was the owner of the largest business enterprise on the island of Cuba. They were married, and she began a wonderful life with her husband... probably only rarely thinking of the man who left her behind, the man who would be a king.

Auburn

You'll find the historic old Auburn in Duncan Park, nestled amongst the oak trees draped with Spanish moss. Although it is an icon of the Old South, it was actually designed by Yankees. A northerner from Massachusetts purchased the land in 1807 for $8000. His name was Lyman Harding, and he would eventually become the very first Attorney General for the state of Mississippi. At the time, though, he wanted a home that would be a showplace.

Harding commissioned Massachusetts architect Levi Weeks to design his home. Levi had migrated from his original home to the city of Natchez around 1808.

The actual construction of Auburn began around 1812, which is confirmed by a letter that was written by Weeks in that year. The letter was addressed to an editor in Boston, and was dated Natchez, September 21, 1812. After describing the business climate in town of the day, Weeks added, "The brick house I am now building is just without the city line and is designed as the most magnificent building in the territory."

The house's two-story portico was very unique for its time, and its stately columns and fan-shaped window over the front door were called "an architect's dream of beauty."

Another architectural feature of the house is a free-standing spiral staircase in the entry hall of the house. It has no support other than at its base. It is rare – one of only a few such stairways in the United States. Others can be found in the Loretto Chapel in Santa Fe, New Mexico, and in the Church of Immaculate Conception in Natchitoches, Louisiana.

The Famous Spiral Staircase

Lyman Harding did not get to enjoy his house for long, however. He passed away in 1820, and seven years later, his estate sold Auburn and the land surrounding it to Dr. Stephen

Duncan for the sum of $20,000. The Duncan family changed the house by adding two symmetrical wings in 1834. They also built a service building and a billiard hall in the side yard. Stephen Duncan was an extremely wealthy man; not only from his medical practice, but also as a planter. He is said to have been one of the largest slaveholders in the South.

While living at Auburn, the Duncans entertained many national celebrities, including Henry Clay, founder of the Whig Party in America. He visited and spent weeks at a time at the house.

An Upstairs Hallway

In 1911, Dr. Duncan's heirs gave Auburn and 210 acres to the city of Natchez as a memorial to the doctor, and that park is named for him. The land surrounding the house became a golf course and a park. While much attention was paid to the park and course, the house was allowed to slowly deteriorate. A decision was made by the city to sell off the exquisite antiques that filled the house so that it could be more easily maintained, and it was opened as a museum for the public to visit.

On March 1st, 1972, the city leased the mansion to a group of ladies with a vision for Auburn – they saw the house restored to its original grandeur and preserved its beauty for future generations of Natchez visitors. The Town and Country Garden Club, which would later become the Auburn Garden Club, took over the responsibilities for the house. The ladies saw their dream come true and today the club oversees and operates Auburn on a volunteer basis.

The house has had a brush with Hollywood; it was used in the 1974 movie *Huckleberry Finn* starring Jeff East and Paul Winfield.

The beautifully restored Auburn is a National Historic Landmark that visitors can tour; proceeds are used for its continued restoration and maintenance.

Auburn
400 Duncan Ave
Natchez, MS 39120
601.442.5981

Monmouth Plantation

The majesty of this antebellum home is evident as you first approach – Monmouth mansion exudes beauty and luxury. Its name comes from Monmouth County in New Jersey, the home of its builder. John Hankinson was the Natchez Postmaster in 1818, constructing this magnificent home for his family. It is a two-story Federal-style brick mansion that was – and is now – one of the showplaces of Natchez.

Unfortunately, Mr. Hankinson only enjoyed his home for seven years. He died of yellow fever in 1825. As the story goes, he and his wife were out riding when they came across a gentleman so weak with sickness that he was leaning up against a post. Feeling sorry for him, they took the poor man in and he died that very night. Only then did they realize that he had passed from Yellow Fever. Both Mr. Hankinson and his wife contracted the disease and soon succumbed to it.

71

In 1820, a twenty-one year-old lawyer and planter named John Anthony Quitman arrived in the city of Natchez. Although he was a rough man who knew how to use his fists, he once said, "In Natchez I must appear as a gentleman, or I cannot be treated as such." He married Eliza Turner in 1824, a lady from a prosperous family. She was the daughter of Judge Turner, an important and influential man in Natchez. The couple's first child was born in 1826. Quitman began looking for a proper home to raise his family, and since Monmouth was available after Mr. Hankinson's death, John Quitman purchased it for the sum of $12,000.

John and his wife Eliza had eleven children. The gentleman of the house led quite an extraordinary life. He served in the high office as Mississippi's Chancellor and then as a state Senator. In 1934 John appointed one of the house slaves, Harry Nichols, to be his personal valet. As it turned out, Harry would accompany Quitman on many of his adventures.

In 1836, John Quitman organized a private militia, the "Fencibles," to fight in the Texas War of Independence from Mexico, and Harry Nichols was at his side. By 1846 Quitman had served as a victorious general in the war.

Because of his reputation Quitman was elected Governor of Mississippi in 1850 and Monmouth became the "White House of Mississippi." As the Civil War slowly seemed to become an unavoidable reality, Quitman was a vocal proponent of the secession of the Southern States. He loved the Southern way of life and was prepared to fight for it. Unfortunately, he died of dysentery at Monmouth in 1858. There have been some rumors that he had been deliberately poisoned at a banquet during the inauguration of President James Buchanan, in Washington, D.C., but it was never proven.

Eliza Quitman died about a year later, leaving Monmouth to their heirs. Daughters Annie Rosalie, J. Antonia, and Louisa married and all remained in residence at Monmouth.

In two years, the Civil War began for Mississippi when the

state seceded from the Union and the men of the house left to fight for the Confederacy. After the city of Natchez surrendered to the Union army, the Monmouth slaves began to run off, leaving the house severely understaffed. The mansion was occupied by Union forces in 1863 and there was extensive looting because of John Quitman's stand for the Confederacy. The three daughters were able to save the house by taking a pledge of loyalty to the United States.

After the war, the Quitman daughters sold off many of the family furnishings to make ends meet while waiting for the Monmouth cotton crops to produce a profit. In 1887 two granddaughters, Eva Lovell and Alice Lovell, moved onto the estate to continue the family tradition.

Years later, in 1914, the last Quitman child, Annie Rosalie Quitman Ducan passed away at Monmouth, and left the estate to her two nieces Eva and Alice. The house and its grounds changed hands several times, but in 1979 two visitors from California named Ronnie and Lani Riches purchased the house with a vision of the beauty that exists there today.

In 1979 it was added to the prestigious National Pilgrimage Corporation; in 1988 it was designated a National Historic Landmark. It has been recommended by Condé Nast and Travel+Leisure magazines, Gourmet Magazine, Zagat Survey and Architectural Digest, and many other publications.

Guests enjoy delicious meals and delightful strolls through the grounds, and Manmouth has become a cornerstone of Natchez hospitality. Visiting Manmouth, it is obvious what John Quitman saw in the house so many years ago.

Monmouth Plantation
36 Melrose Avenue
Natchez MS, 39120
800.828.4531
www.monmouthplantation.com

Outlaws of the Trace

Outlaws, Scalawags, Ruffians or Land Pirates – no matter what you call them, they were the scourge of innocent people who were traveling the Natchez Trace. No one was safe from these predators.

Some were just common criminals, there one day, gone the next, but others made legendary names for themselves: Joseph Hare, Micajah ("Big") Harpe, Wiley ("Little") Harpe, Samuel Mason and John Murrell.

With Natchez as the endpoint of the trail, on any given evening you might find any of these ruffians in an Under-the-Hill saloon or bordello – when they weren't out prowling the Trace, that is.

There are countless tales about these notorious bandits and

their exploits that grew through the years; I can't guarantee that every word I am writing in this chapter is accurate. I can only assure you that these tales were told to me as the truth, and I'll pass them on with that caveat.

Joseph Hare, The Gentleman Bandit

Joseph is certainly one of the more interesting of the Trace outlaws. Born Joseph Thompson Hare in Philadelphia, PA, he was apprenticed into the tailor trade, which must have made quite an impression on him – he never gave up his love of clothing and costumes.

He found that the life of a criminal also held an allure, and before long Joseph had a dossier of petty crimes under his belt. To avoid getting into too much trouble, he decided to head south for new horizons. He ended up in the city of New Orleans, where he soon went back to his criminal ways.

Expanding his territory, Hare discovered Natchez and the Trace. He added a few men to his gang and began to prey on travelers – especially merchants carrying either goods to sell, or cash from transactions they'd already conducted.

Joseph Hare and his gang used many tactics in their robbing. On some occasions, they would rub berry juice on their hands and face to give themselves a grotesque appearance to frighten their victims all the more, discouraging any heroics.

Some reports say that the bandits would dress up as Indians, prompting the people being robbed to report the Chickasaw or the Choctaw as the culprits.

Others say that Hare was always dressed in his finest, being dapper and polite during the robberies – a perfect gentleman.

After a particularly profitable spell, the gang reportedly traveled to New Orleans, where they hosted a cotillion for the finest people in town. Later, when he was captured by the Spanish, several people that had attended the cotillion wrote letters attesting to Hare's magnanimous stature in the community and helped to free him.

Whatever the case, there is no doubt that Joseph Hare was a Natchez Trace bandit. His favorite hideout was a cave near Natchez, where he would trade with both the Indians and the town's citizenry. He employed an Indian maid named Hay Foot, who scouted for them when they were on the Trace looking for prospective victims. During his cave days, Hare started a diary where he recorded his thoughts; one entry says:

"Let not any one be induced to turn highwayman by reading this book and seeing the great sums of money I have robbed, for it is a desperate life, full of danger, and sooner or later ends at the gallows."

Hare was eventually captured. He was running from a posse when he was stopped in his tracks by the vision of a brilliant, shining white horse in the trail before him. It so disturbed him that he stopped to contemplate the event, and the posse caught up with him.

Convinced that this was divine intervention, he spent the next five years in prison reading the Bible and preaching to anyone who would listen to him. He was sure that the white horse had been a vision of Jesus, come to change his evil ways. It appeared that Hare had done just that and he was finally released.

Within a year, however, he picked up his gun again and returned to his old criminal ways by robbing a mail coach.

Some say that Hare was arrested for the final time at a tailor's shop in Baltimore, as he was shopping for another debonair suit. Although he tried to escape his fate using every legal means possible, on the morning of September 10, 1818, Joseph Thompson Hare's death sentence was carried out there in Maryland. He was hanged by the neck until dead, as fifteen hundred spectators looked on. It was the end of one of the most famous outlaws of the Natchez Trace.

Samuel Mason, the River Pilot

Along with being a bandit of the Natchez Trace, Samuel Mason is credited with founding the famous Cave-in-Rock on the Ohio River. The cavern was twenty-five feet wide, fifteen feet high, and one hundred and fifty feet long; it was perfect for hiding a band of outlaws. The cave overlooked the river from a high bluff, and the opening was camouflaged by trees and brush. From the cave, however, a lookout would have a perfect view of the river in both directions. It was a perfect place to prey on the flatboats that transported cargo and passengers of the day.

Samuel Mason first set up shop at Cave-in-Rock in 1797. He was referred to as "Captain Mason," but no one knows whether it came from his military service, or the fact that he hijacked many ships on the river and became the "captain" of the small vessels.

He used many strategic tactics for his piracy. For example, he put a large sign on the riverbank that read *Liquor Vault and House of Entertainment*, something that would be very attractive to the men traveling the river. As the boats stopped for the crew to wet their whistle, Mason and his men would bushwhack them and take their possessions.

Mason sometimes employed the services of a woman that he would station on Hurricane Island, which was a short distance from Cave-in-Rock. She would call out to passing vessels as if she was stranded and after they picked her up, she would direct the boat to land near the cave where Mason and his river pirates would be waiting.

If the boat was heavy with cargo, Samuel Mason would often kill everyone on board; he and his outlaw band would then take control. The murdered crew would be slit open, filled with rocks, and then submerged in the river – a trick that he learned from the notorious Harpe brothers. The cargo and boat would be taken down to New Orleans, where they would be sold.

Mason and crew would return to their cave by taking the Natchez Trace, where they found travelers to be easy picking along the way. After several years of preying on river travelers, in 1799 Mason abandoned his river piracy, and focused strictly on the Trace for his thievery. This may have been his downfall.

One or more of his men eventually betrayed him for the bounty money and presented his head to the local authorities... but that's a story that I'll save until the next section.

Big Harpe and Little Harpe

Micajah and Wiley Harpe were known as "Big Harpe" and "Little Harpe," respectively – the notorious Harpe brothers. Some say that they were actually first cousins, while others say that they weren't related at all. No matter how – or if – they were related, the Harpes left a trail of death and destruction wherever they went.

The pair started out as farmers in Knoxville, Tennessee, living in the countryside with their wives. They soon found that it was easier to steal the livestock of their neighbors than to raise the animals themselves.

When a local farmer took exception to his hogs and horses being stolen, he chased the Harpes and their families out of town, and their killing spree began. The "brothers" holed up in a wayside tavern for the evening, and had an encounter with a man named Johnson that angered the duo. They murdered the man, slit his gut open and filled his body with stones before sinking it in a river – a modus operandi that would become common with their victims.

If anyone had a doubt at all about the Harpes, it was settled with an atrocity that defied all understanding. They took a young girl prisoner near the Green River area and brutally killed her by bashing her head against the bridge railing until she was dead. So began the terrible story of the Harpe brothers.

They made their way up and down the Natchez Trace, robbing some travelers, while simply murdering others in cold blood and leaving their belongings with their bodies.

At some point they acquired another "wife" that the two men shared, bringing their party to five adults and various children that the women had birthed over the years. Several times the Harpe brothers put their own children to death so that they wouldn't be slowed down by the infants.

The general public was shocked and disgusted by the exploits of the duo, but soon even the most heinous "Trace pirates" would turn their backs on the Harpes. While hiding out at the legendary Cave-in-Rock on the Ohio River, Big Harpe grabbed an innocent man who'd been traveling on the river, and forced him to strip off his clothes. Harpe then tied his victim to a horse, which he proceeded to blindfold – the horse, not the man. Finally, he took the horse and its captive rider to the top of the bluff above the cave, and drove it running toward the edge. He laughed as the steed and its rider went over the edge, to die a horrible death on the rocks below.

The Harpe brothers and their families were soon shunned by outlaws and honest citizens alike. A price was on their heads, and the brothers assumed that it would eventually be claimed.

The beginning of the end came when the Harpe families sought refuge at the home of an acquaintance named Moses Stegall. The man of the house wasn't home, but his wife offered them a place to spend the night, as she had done another friend, Major William Love, who had arrived earlier. The Harpe wives learned from Mrs. Stegall that she kept a savings of $40.00 at the house in case of an emergency, and they immediately told their husbands. Big and Little Harpe acted quickly – in the dead of the night, they murdered Major Love, Mrs. Stegall, and the Stegall's four-month-old infant boy. When they left the house, the Harpes put a torch to it hoping to destroy all the evidence.

When Mr. Stegall returned home, he was overcome with grief and anger. It didn't take long for all signs to point to Big and Little Harpe; he quickly organized a posse to go after them.

Judgment day came for Micajah, Big Harpe, in August of 1799. The Harpe brothers had left their wives at a safe place, and had split up to try to improve their chances for escape. Big Harpe found himself cornered by the posse. Out of ammunition, he sat down on a rock and watched as Mr. Stegall approached.

Here the story varies. One version says that Stegall shot Big Harpe dead, while another indicates that the final sentence was carried out while Harpe was still alive. There is no doubt that Mr. Stegall took a knife and removed the head of Big Harpe, and placed it in a tree on the road for everyone to see. It was a warning to all bandits that times were becoming more civilized – random violence would not be tolerated. To this day, that location is called "Harpe's Head."

No one knows for sure whether or not Little Harpe ever knew the fate of his brother, but you would have to assume that he'd have heard the story at some point in the next four years – because that's how long he managed to elude the law.

Little Harpe made his way back to Cave-in-Rock and joined an outlaw band ruled by a rogue named Captain Samual Mason. They terrorized the Trace for years, although eventually Little Harpe and a companion named James May decided to sell out their leader. They jumped Mason, killed him, and removed his head, an ironic, unintentional nod to Big Harpe's demise.

Harpe and May took Mason's head to the local sheriff to claim the reward money, but while they were there, a victim of one of their robberies on the Trace walked in. It was a one-in-million coincidence. The man recognized the pair, identified them immediately, and the sheriff took Harpe and May into custody. Although they managed to escape, a posse was quickly formed to hunt them down.

They were soon captured, and in January 1804, Little Harpe and James May were executed by hanging. The heads of the two outlaws were placed on stakes on the Trace as a warning to other criminals.

The story of Big Harpe and Little Harpe ended there – both beheaded, and used as deterrents to crime on the Natchez Trace. But what of the Harpe women? Although they had been left for safekeeping, the women and their children were taken into custody. They were finally released, under the premise that they'd suffered enough by living with the Harpe Brothers.

The Two Faces of John Murrell

John A. Murrell was a tortured man; ruled by his desire for money on one hand and his religious upbringing on the other. He was considered to be one of the most dangerous outlaws of the Natchez Trace.

His split personality started early in life. Born in Tennessee in 1804, his father was a Methodist preacher who traveled the countryside spreading the Word. While his dad was gone, his mother made ends meet by teaching the kids to steal for whatever the family needed.

This duality between good and bad carried over into his adult years. He robbed travelers along the Natchez Trace, sometimes preaching them a sermon in the process.

At times when he traveled with a gang, Murrell would stop at churches and pose as a traveling minister. He would ingratiate himself with the preacher, and would invariably be invited to give the Sunday sermon.

As John Murrell whipped the congregation into a frenzy with his words of fire and brimstone, members of his gang would be outside the church, ransacking the buggies and stealing the horses. Mark Twain left his own account of this

81

particular practice of Murrell: "When he traveled, his usual disguise was that of an itinerant preacher; and it is said that his discourses were very 'soul-moving' – interesting the hearers so much that they forgot to look after their horses, which were carried away by his confederates while he was preaching."

Murrell would also pass himself off as an Abolitionist – a champion of slaves' rights. In reality though, it was all a masterful, criminal plan. The Reverend John would help a slave escape, then sell the slave to a new owner. After a few days he would facilitate the man's escape again, finding a new owner to sell him to. This pattern would continue until the slave became known in the area and was no longer a viable commodity. At that point, Murrell would simply kill the man and bury his body or sink it in the river. As the story goes, he and his band of men would be controlling any number of "freed" slaves at any given time, all of which would eventually come to a tragic end.

The number of outlaws that Murrell had at his disposal is subject to debate. The numbers range from a handful of marauders to over two thousand bandits roaming the Mississippi River and the Natchez Trace. The actual figure will never be known, but there is no dispute of the preacher-outlaw's treacherous reputation.

The pinnacle of John Murrell's career was going to be an uprising of slaves, who would free themselves from their masters at an appointed time. They would take over the plantations of the South, and install Murrell as their potentate of the Louisiana and Mississippi area.

Before he could put his plan into effect, the bandit was apprehended by authorities as he tried to steal a boat loaded with cargo.

Murrell was sentenced to prison for ten years, and when he was finally released, his contemporaries had either died, moved on, or been sent to jail themselves. With no one to lead or work with he turned to a life of farming before his death a few years later.

His reputation never gave him rest, though – after Murrell's death, his body was dug up by bandits in order to claim a bounty on his skull. His thumbs were also taken, and one of them is in the possession of the Tennessee State Museum. Presumably, the rest of John Murrell's body was left in the grave, a terrible ending to a life split between good and evil.

The Devil's Punchbowl

When one first hears mention about the Devil's Punchbowl, it sounds like the stuff of urban legend; a great story, really – a cone-shaped crater where a meteorite came crashing down to Earth eons ago, leaving traces of space rocks that cast a strange, magnetic field over the area.

As steamboats began to navigate the Mississippi, captains reported that their compasses behaved erratically when passing by the area. It didn't take long for the notorious river pirates in the area to take advantage of that confusion – they would hide nearby, preying on the boats that were momentarily disoriented. Some stories go as far as to say that some bandits even made the Devil's Punchbowl their hideout. With its steep walls and thick foliage, it would certainly have been a great hiding place.

All those stories are local legend, but documentation about

the Punchbowl does exist. One such place is an old book, *In Old Natchez* by Catharine Van Court, published by Doubleday, Doran & Co, Inc in 1937:

About a mile north of Natchez there is a driveway walled in by steep embankments; the trees above it are matted with moss and tropical creepers. Their interlacing branches form a leafy roof over this road which leads to Clermont Plantation, from which place the Devil's Punch Bowl may be seen. This Bowl is one of nature's freaks and is similar in formation to the one on the Isle of Elba, where Napoleon was a prisoner. It, too, was called the Devil's Punch bowl.

The Natchez bowl is a gigantic, semicircular pit which looks as though it had been made by a tremendous, inverted cone that had burrowed into the bluffs. It covers many acres and slowly enlarges each year. The center seems to have dropped out of that portion of creation, but ancient forest trees cling to the Bowl's precipitous edges. The soil is rich loam, or silt, and is free from any form of stone.

More than a century ago a writer said of the hills just above the Bowl:

They are properly the head or termination of the eastern highland of the United States... the antennae of the Alleghenies. The hypothesis that they were once promontories, with waves of the Mexican Gulf breaking at their feet, has the support of many scientists.

The earthquake of 1811 which destroyed New Madrid, Mo., and formed Reelfoot Lake in Tennessee, caused no perceptible change in the Punch Bowl; these hills must have been thrown over the primitive formation by some extraordinary upheaval or convulsion long before that time.

The Natchez Indians evidently made use of the Bowl, for their mounds are numerous near its mouth; vestiges of pottery and skeletons are there to tell the story.

85

There are countless traditions connected with this uncanny spot. Some tell of river pirates, runaway slaves, buried treasure, romance and adventure. One story is that a great meteor containing radium and other precious substances fell here and not only buried itself fathoms deep but took with it many acres of woodland. In support of this theory, river men assert, the magnetic compass is greatly disturbed at this point; some even say the needle spins completely around. Farfetched as this story may seem, many in the vicinity give it credence, while others advance the idea that hidden treasure in huge metal containers is buried there. Much vain digging for piratical gold has taken place in the basin of the great Bowl.

Ms. Van Court's account of the Punchbowl mirrored the local legends, so they at least go back over seventy years.

Another text on the Devil's Punchbowl comes from the book *Natchez On The Mississippi* by Harnett T. Kane, published by William Morrow & Company in 1947:

Along the river just outside Natchez, [the outlaw Samuel] Mason had his eye on a point of new operation – a peculiar, to some awesome, phenomenon called, "The Devil's Punchbowl." Far in the past, a great cup-shaped hole, about five hundred feet wide, had formed in the soft earth of the river bluffs. Slowly it seemed to widen, as gullies formed along its sides and rows of trees hurtled into its depths. Thickly grown, it provided a dim, almost impenetrable place of concealment. Natives thought that a heavy meteor might once have plummeted here, sinking into the earth. Steamboat men claimed that their compasses behaved crazily when they passed.

Inevitably the "Punchbowl" became a spot to be gossiped about, and feared. Hundreds were certain the vicinity contained buried gold; at intervals men with picks and shovels climbed warily about it. Early Spanish and French pirates were supposed to have secreted their treasures in the depths. Daring runaway slaves headed there and hid for days. Through the years men who had reason to dodge their fellows headed to the "Punchbowl."

By this time [the outlaw] Sam Mason went to work. Here he established several intelligent assistants and coached them. At the water's edge they posed as farmers, holding up produce for the flatboatmen. Or one might cry piteously for help, saying he was being beaten to death. Sometimes a girl was assigned to the task; nothing stirred folks like the shriek of a female. Once the fools stepped on shore, a few hatchet strokes did the rest. The naked bodies were hauled to the edge of the Bowl and sent hurtling down. Sometimes Mason's men would start a couple of them moving at the same time, and bet which corpse would hit first. For years the Masonites slipped in and out of the Punchbowl.

Mr. Kane had similar stories, with an even more elaborate account of the outlaw aspect to the Devil's Punchbowl.

To find it, one must only travel north on Cemetery Road, pass the Natchez City Cemetery, then the National Cemetery. The road finally begins to narrow and turns from pavement into dirt. Slow down and watch the landscape on the left side, and suddenly there it will be... the Devil's Punchbowl.

Make no mistake – it is a treacherous place. Do not try to explore the Punchbowl, because you will most likely get hurt... it looks like a place that invites serious injury. The fragile loess soil along the edges easily gives way. The walls of the Devil's Punchbowl are extremely steep, and a person wouldn't be likely to survive a fall from the very top. It is probably that danger that made it such a good hideout for villains in the past.

The Southern Slope of the Devil's Punchbowl

The photograph above shows the slope at the edge of the bowl, and beyond the trees in the foreground is the shady far edge. This might be more evident in the picture at the first of the chapter, which also shows the opening to the river on the west side – getting a good photo is a challenge, because as Mr. Kane said in his book, "…rows of trees hurtled into its depths. Thickly grown, it provided a dim, almost impenetrable place of concealment."

Such a terrain would definitely be attractive to anyone seeking to hide out from the law, which makes a strong case for the notorious side of the place. The stories of the outlaws who frequented the Bowl could certainly be true – the river pirates were common visitors to Natchez Under-the-Hill, which is just a mile away. Today, however, most people are content just to stop their car and take a peek into the bowels of the Devil's Punchbowl from the safety of the road.

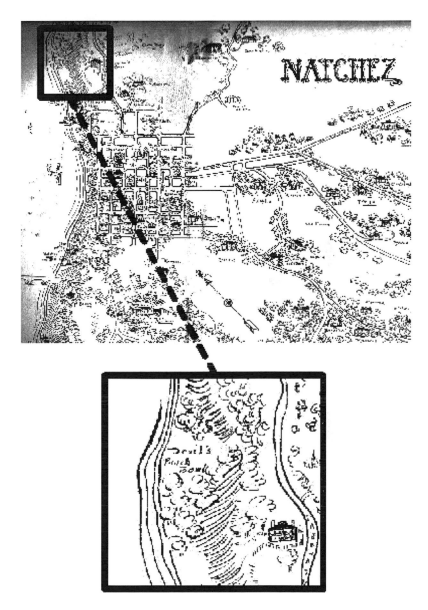

A hand-drawn map of Natchez showing the location of the
Devil's Punchbowl, from the book, *A Day in Natchez* by
Theodora Britton Marshall and Gladys Crail Evans, 1946.

Skeptics believe that the round shape of the Punchbowl is just a geometrical happenstance caused by a whirlpool in the river centuries ago, and cone-shape was a factor of the water level slowly going down as the soil was eroded. On the other hand, who knows for sure about the origin of the Devil's Punchbowl? It is certainly fun to entertain the notion of a prehistoric meteorite crashing down from the heavens, and perhaps frightening a dinosaur or two in the process.

Rosalie Mansion

Fort Rosalie is long gone, but today you will find a stately mansion standing in the place where the old fortress looked out over the river. The house shares the fort's name, in fact – a tribute to that origin of the city.

The story of Rosalie Mansion begins back at the turn of the 19th century when a man named Peter Little arrived in Natchez from Pittsburgh, Pennsylvania. He was quite an entrepreneur, developing a sawmill run by steam to take advantage of the large tracts of timber across the Mississippi River. His was the first sawmill in the Natchez area, and he soon became a wealthy businessman.

As Peter traveled back and forth across the Mississippi River to manage his timber dealings, he became friends with the man who operated the ferryboat, Jacob Lowe. Although it was an odd pairing, but because of their constant contact the

91

two men came to be close companions.

In 1806, Peter was devastated to hear that both Jacob and his wife had contracted yellow fever, and were not expected to live. On their deathbeds, each asked that Peter look after their thirteen-year-old daughter Eliza.

He promised to do so, and to accomplish this, Peter Little married Eliza Lowe that very year – in name only – and immediately sent her off to school in Baltimore, Maryland.

When her education was complete she returned to Natchez, and Peter took her to New Orleans for a honeymoon – he outfitted her in the fashions of the time, then returned home. Peter presented Eliza to Natchez society as his wife.

As their fortune increased over the years, Peter decided to build a mansion for his wife. He paid around $3000.00 for the area on the bluff that was known as the "Old Fort." It was the location of Fort Rosalie, named for the Duchess de Pontchartrain, and was the site of the Natchez Indian massacre that occurred in 1729. Little decided to call the mansion "Rosalie" in honor of the old fort.

It was designed by Peter's brother-in-law James S. Griffin, who came to Natchez from Baltimore. He envisioned a Federal-style home, a two-story brick structure. There are two porches, or galleries, on both stories in front and in back, lined with Doric pillars. Mr. Griffin designed a simple floor plan, with two parlors on one side of the main hall downstairs and a dining room and library on the other. That design is mirrored upstairs, with two bedrooms on each side of the upper hallway. Construction started in 1820, and the mansion was complete in 1823. The materials used in construction were of local cypress and mahogany that Mr. Little imported, all of which was cut in his local sawmill. He insisted that only the best materials were used in construction of the house; much of the hand-carved woodwork was done by slave labor.

Rosalie's kitchen was built away from the main house because of the threat of fire. The outdoor kitchen was located in the two-story brick dependency building behind the house. All food was prepared in the kitchen's fireplace, then carried in covered dishes through the latticed passage and handed to dining room servants through the window into the main house.

A Formal Parlor At Rosalie

Back to Peter and Eliza; the couple had a very happy life at Rosalie until Eliza's death in 1853. Although Peter's heart was broken, he lived for about another three years and died in December of 1856. Without heirs, he had never bothered to draft a will other than the original, which left his possessions to Eliza; upon his death, the fate of this magnificent mansion was terrible – it was simply put up for public auction.

Rosalie was then purchased by Andrew Wilson, and at that time most of the Little furnishings had been dispersed. Wilson then brought in fine furnishings from the eastern U.S.

and as far as from Europe. His wife and their adopted daughter Fannie traveled to New York and brought back twenty pieces of Belter furniture, which remain in the house to this day. The collection is one of the finest sets of John Henry Belter furniture in the nation, and is a showpiece for Rosalie.

During the Wilson years came the Civil War, and in an ironic twist of fate, Rosalie was the first name of the young girl, Rosalie Beekman, who was the only war casualty from an attack on the city. Rosalie and her family were fleeing up Silver Street when the federal gunboat U.S.S. Essex shelled Natchez on September 2nd, 1862. She died the next day.

Rosalie's Fine Furnishings

Prior to the Yankee occupation of Natchez, Mrs. Wilson had ordered her slaves to take the French gold-leaf mirrors down, wrap them in blankets and hide them in a cave in the bluffs below the city where they would be protected by bales of cotton. The mirrors weathered the war well and were eventually brought back to the house. To this day the mirrors have never been refinished – they're still as beautiful as they were over one hundred years ago.

During the war Rosalie was occupied by Northern Troops. Fortunately, the officer in charge was General Walter Gresham, whose appreciation of the house probably saved it. He issued an order that the delicate furniture be locked up in the attic where it would all be safe.

In the course of the war and the occupation of Rosalie, only the dining room was damaged. It was used as the Union mess hall, and meals were cooked in the fireplace. Today you can still see the cracks and stains in the marble from that time.

General Ulysses S. Grant stayed at Rosalie while he was visiting Natchez, and one of the upstairs rooms contains the desk on which he signed his letter to General Sherman giving him direction to start his terrible march across the south.

You would think that the Northern occupation of the house would be remembered as a very bad time, but after the war, Mrs. Gresham – the general's wife – and Mrs. Wilson remained in touch, writing back and forth like two old friends.

In 1938 Rosalie was purchased by the Mississippi State Society Daughters of the American Revolution. Descendants of the Wilson family were still living in the house, though, so the agreement allowed them to remain there until their death. Wilson family members lived in the house until 1958.

In the years that followed, the ladies of the D.A.R. have been the caretakers and restorers of Rosalie, kindly sharing the mansion, its gardens and history with the public.

Rosalie Mansion
100 Orleans St
Natchez, MS 39120
601.445.4555
www.rosaliemansion.com

The Birth of the Bowie Knife

When most people think of Colonel James Bowie and his famous knife, their thoughts take them about five hundred miles west of Natchez, to a place called Mission San Antonio de Valero – or, as we know it today, The Alamo.

You can probably close your eyes and see Bowie fighting Santa Anna's army in the closing hours of the battle by courageously swinging that famous blade.

Something that a lot of people don't know, however, is that Bowie's knife was baptized in battle not far from Natchez, in what historians would eventually come to call *The Sandbar Fight*.

The hostility began a year before in Alexandria, when Bowie confronted Major Norris Wright, sheriff of Rapides Parish, in a barroom. Bowie had been informed that Wright had been spreading disparaging remarks around town about him, and the big man was not one to stand by for such insults to his character.

Sheriff Wright was involved in a card game in Bailey's Hotel, when Bowie charged in. Although Bowie was unarmed, the sheriff produced a pistol and shot him at point-blank range. Before he fell, Bowie managed to bite off one of Wright's fingers, and even lost a tooth in the process.

Although an up-close pistol shot would kill any ordinary man, Bowie somehow survived, and perhaps even thrived. Historians speculate that perhaps there was a misfire, or that the Colonel had a book in his pocket that received the brunt of the shot, but whatever the case James Bowie was no worse for wear. Although he did not seek immediate retaliation, an animosity continued between Norris Wright and Bowie.

James Bowie

One thing about the encounter changed Mr. Bowie, however. He would never be caught unarmed again. From that day on, he wore a large hunting knife – which some people described as a butcher's knife – on a custom scabbard on his belt.

As the next year unfolded, two Alexandria gentlemen named Dr. Thomas Maddox and Mr. Samuel Wells had a disagreement that started with a bit of unsavory gossip about Wells' sister, Mary Sibley. A gentleman's challenge to a duel was issued, but since laws had been passed to restrict such behavior, the pair chose the city of Natchez to settle their differences. By taking their duel to a sandbar in the Mississippi River, they would escape the laws of both Louisiana and Mississippi – the event was slated for September 19, 1827.

In such an orchestrated event, each man would have a "second," a man who bore specific responsibilities; these ranged from acting as an arbitrator in verbal negotiations, to standing in for his principal in the dual under specified circumstances. Major George C. McWhorter served as the second to Samuel Wells, and Dr. Maddox's second was Colonel Robert Crain. Each had a physician to accompany their group to the sandbar, Doctors Richard Cuny and James Denny, to attend any wounds inflicted in the conflict.

A Typical Sandbar On The Mississippi River

Other men accompanying each side remained on the banks of the river. For Dr. Maddox, this included Major Norris

98

Wright, the nemesis of James Bowie, and Alfred and Carey Blanchard.

Friends of Samuel Wells also waited in watching distance, and they included his younger brother Thomas, General Samuel Cuny, and Colonel Bowie.

On the sandbar, the first duel took place just after noon. The men stood eight paces apart, left side to left side, and upon the command "fire," raised their weapons and discharged them. Both missed, leaving each unharmed.

A gentlemen's duel required two volleys, however, so even though the seconds gave an impassioned plea to call the challenge a draw, a second firing was set.

The pair fired again, and once more missed. With honor satisfied, they shook hands, declaring the disagreement to be settled. At that point, the entire event should have been over, and all parties would gather at a Natchez bar to toast the resolution without bloodshed.

What happened next is open to the conjecture and interpretation of history. As the men on the sandbar started walking toward the shore, the two parties of men on either side came out of the brush to meet them.

When the two groups confronted each other, all were carrying weapons. General Samuel Cuny, who had a lingering disagreement with Colonel Robert Crain, suggested that the two of them settle their differences in a duel of their own.

Crain thought that their confrontation might take place right on the spot, so he leveled the dueling pistols that he held, and things began to escalate.

Dr. Richard Cuny stepped between the two men, and the tension was momentarily alleviated. But not far from them, Colonel Robert Crain saw James Bowie advancing, pointed a pistol at him, and pulled the trigger… the melee of the sandbar then ensued.

Reportedly, Bowie called out, "Crain, you have shot me, and I will kill you if I can!"

A volley of fire ensued from the different men on both sides, and Bowie was seen unsheathing his massive knife and charging toward Colonel Crain.

The Colonel threw his empty pistol at Bowie, who collapsed when it hit him in the head. Crain ran for shelter in the trees, but Major Norris Wright sought to do in his old foe. He charged Bowie, and as the fight escalated, Bowie drew his massive knife, burying it in Wright, who fell limp.

Wrestling out from under the dead man, Bowie continued to wield his knife against his attackers.

When it was all over two men were dead, including Wright, and at least four admitted to being wounded. The newspapers had a field day with the duel, which would soon be encapsulated with the battle afterwards to an event dubbed "The Sandbar Fight."

With that small skirmish, Colonel James Bowie and his legendary knife were both launched into the fabric of American history.

Forks of the Road

A visit to "Forks of the Road" is a somber experience. This was the second-largest slave market in the South outside of New Orleans. Between the years of 1810 and 1863, over 200,000 slaves were bought and sold at the Forks of the Road. Human lives were bartered for money, land, or other gain; families were broken up and sold to rival plantations along the Mississippi; chains kept the slaves together on the auction block, and punishment was meted out with ferocity.

As you read the information kiosk, its initial words are chilling: *You are standing at Forks of the Road, the site of several markets where enslaved humans were bought and sold from the 1830s until 1863. This was the center of the trade in Natchez, one of the busiest slave trading towns in the nation.*

The very idea of slavery seems barbaric and inhuman in society today, but in pre-Civil War Natchez, it was the order of the day. As the population grew in the city so did the number of slaves. Some were brought along with other property as their masters purchased plantations in the area, while others were sold as surplus from plantations in Kentucky, Maryland, and Virginia. According to the kiosk at the site, more than 750,000 enslaved African-Americans were moved to the lower South region of the U.S. between 1800 and 1860. This idea, that of being "sold South," was so detestable that some escaped and ran north, while others implored their neighbors to purchase them. A few even resorted to self-mutilation, cutting off a hand, arm, or foot, to make themselves impractical for sale.

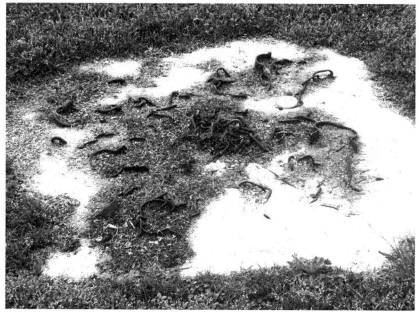

A Display Of Slavery Shackles At The Site

The flow of slaves into Natchez continued through the years, though, and by 1860, slaves were three quarters of the population in the area. Natchez also contained free black men who owned slaves themselves; one was William Johnson who is profiled in the *Murder of the Natchez Barber* chapter of this book.

A majority of the slaves sold in Natchez were auctioned at the Forks of the Road – it was a terrible place. In the book *The Southwest by a Yankee* by Joseph Holt Ingraham, published in 1834, the author writes, *"A mile from Natchez, we came to a cluster of rough wooden buildings in the angle of two roads... Entering through a wide gate into a narrow court-yard, partially enclosed by low buildings, a scene of novel character was at once presented. A line of negroes, commencing at the entrance... extended in a semicircle around the right side of the yard... they stood perfectly still, and in close order, while some gentlemen were passing from one to another examining for the purpose of buying."*

Slave-traders brought their wares to the Forks of the Road on three different routes:

- The road from Virginia to Natchez was the least expensive, but was extremely laborious for those on foot;
- Arriving by river from New Orleans, after being shipped across the Atlantic, which cost about $20 per slave;
- Coming downriver from Missouri or Kentucky, which was fast and cheap.

In 1808, Congress had banned the importation of any more slaves from Africa, which increased the value of enslaved people already within the boundary of the United States. These price increases were certainly reflected on the auction block at the Forks of the Road.

In 1846, former slave, abolitionist, editor, orator, author, statesman and reformer Frederick Douglas described the institution of slavery as follows: *"The slave has no rights; he is a being with all the capacities of a man in the conditions of the brute. Such is the slave in the American plantations. He can decide no question relative to his own actions; the slave-holder*

103

decides what he shall eat or drink, when and to whom he shall speak, when he shall work, and how long he shall work; when he shall marry... what is right and wrong, virtue and vice. The slave-holder becomes the sole disposer of the mind, soul and body of his slave..."

Actual Slavery Newspaper Advertisement

Forks of the Road was last used for slave trading in 1863. During the Union occupation, troops used the buildings as a refugee camp for newly freed slaves. The buildings were razed when the Union occupation was over, ending the dreadful legacy of the Forks of the Road.

In 1995, African-American activists began an effort to preserve the Forks of the Road area as a historic site. It has been included in the National Underground Railroad Network to Freedom, and in 2000, First Lady Hilary Rodham Clinton's White House Millennium Council officially recognized Forks of the Road. You can find out more about this historic place by visiting the website below – with its tragic history, it is still an important part of our culture today.

www.forksoftheroads.net

The Murder of the Natchez Barber

Everyone loves a good murder mystery, and in this case, we have a murder – but it is certainly no mystery. The victim identified the killer on his deathbed and the authorities took him into custody. Because of an unfortunate set of circumstances, however, the murderer would never be convicted of the crime... but I'm getting ahead of myself. Long before that end to the story, it is much more important – and interesting – to look at how it began.

William Johnson was born into slavery in 1809 to a mulatto slave mother and a white father, presumably his owner Captain William Johnson, after whom the boy was named. It was highly unlikely that he would escape the life of servitude, much less become a well-respected, wealthy Natchez businessman, but such was the case of William Johnson.

He won his emancipation in 1820 after his master – and most likely, father – petitioned the matter to the Mississippi legislature. Prior to that date, Captain Johnson had secured the freedom of William's mother Amy and sister Adelia.

A free black man living in the South prior to the Civil War was held to a different set of laws than his white counterparts. He could not vote in an election, hold any sort of public office, serve in the military, or testify against a white person in court.

Still, William was determined to be successful in life, and took an apprenticeship at his brother-in-law James Miller's barbershop. After learning the trade, he opened a shop of his own in Port Gibson, Mississippi, in the late 1820s.

In 1830, he bought his brother-in-law's Natchez barbershop for three hundred dollars and began to teach the trade to free black boys – many of whom later took paying positions with him.

William Johnson soon parlayed his three hundred dollar investment to over three thousand, and he had established himself as a prominent citizen in Natchez' free black community. In 1835, the eligible young bachelor was noticed by twenty-year-old Ann Battles, a free black woman, and they were soon married. About six months after that, he began a diary of everyday life in Natchez, which he would continue for the rest of his life.

The entries in the diary told not only of the barbershop business, but also of the goings on around town and his own personal amusements. William was a hunter and fisherman, and he chronicled his excursions with other free black men of the time. Like many men of the day, he enjoyed betting on horseracing – those exploits are contained in the diary as well, along with news from books and papers of the day.

In his first entry of paying taxes, he acknowledged owning four slaves at a value of $1,655. This was quite a paradox – a black man owning black slaves – but in the South, all successful businessmen owned slaves, and William wanted to be successful.

When a destructive tornado hit downtown Natchez on May 7, 1840, it was a terrible time for the city. This was the second deadliest tornado in United States history, killing 317 people and injuring 109. It was one of the few such events to kill more people than it injured.

Although the family suffered no loss of life, William collected bricks, windows and doors from buildings that were destroyed and built a new home on land owned by his mother-in-law on State Street. The interior walls were finished with plaster that had been reinforced with human hair from his barbershops around town.

As William's holdings expanded, he purchased 700 acres south of Natchez and several more slaves to farm cotton on the land. It was not necessarily a profitable venture, but he did gain more status as a slave-owning cotton farmer.

William and Ann's family grew and by 1850 they had eleven children. All were home-schooled; the oldest four had been sent away to New Orleans to acquire a higher education. By this time, William owned several barbershops and was considered one of the most successful businessmen in Natchez.

He leant money to white entrepreneurs, rented out commercial real estate, and operated a hauling business using his slaves. Still, his main sources of income were the barbershops; they were staffed with black workers, catering to the white clientele. The furnishings in each shop were plush and comfortable. People began to refer to William Johnson as "The Barber of Natchez." All this time, he chronicled his life in his diaries.

William's life was cut short, unfortunately, by the murder that I mentioned at the start of this chapter. It seems that William Johnson and his neighbor Baylor Winn, also a free black man, had a dispute over their property line. Like any gentlemen of the day, they presented the matter for the courts to decide, and the judge ruled in William's favor.

This didn't end the matter for Baylor Winn, though, and the events are best described in this newspaper article of the day:

Dreadful Murder in Natchez
From The Concordian Intelligencier
Natchez, Mississippi
June 21, 1851

On Monday evening last, just at dusk, as Mr. William Johnson, an esteemed citizen, and long known as the proprietor of the fashionable barber's shop on Main Street, when returning from his plantation, a few miles from the city, was fired upon and killed from the road side. He was accompanied by two or three young persons, one of them being his son. The oldest boy with him, named Hoggatt, was desperately wounded by the same shot; as well as two of the horses with the party. Johnson was seen to fall, as if killed instantly and the rest of the party, the wounded boy with them, made as rapid flight as they could to Natchez, and gave the alarm. Dr. Blackburn, in his carriage, instantly repaired to the spot and found Johnson lying on his face apparently insensible. On turning him over, he groaned; and when the Doctor gave him some cordial, he revived sufficiently to speak. The first words announced the name of his murderer, as also did his last, as he died, in great distress, at his family residence at two o'clock the following morning.

About an hour after Johnson's death, Mr. Baylor Winn, a planter, living some seven miles below Natchez, was arrested by officers Dillon and Benbrook, and brought to the city jail. The officers were accompanied by Messrs. W. Rotrammel, John Munce, N. Strickland and B. Massey; but no resistance to the process was made, and the prisoner surrendered himself

---

without any remark, or appearance either of fear or surprise. The boy Hoggatt still lingers in a most precarious condition, with but little hope of his life. Johnson was shot through the left lobe of the lungs, and the boy in the abdomen.

The court of examination before the Justices will commence this morning at the Natchez Court House, and will no doubt be attended by many hundreds. Both parties being in good pecuniary circumstances, the best lawyers of the Natchez bar have been arrayed, either for the prosecution or the defense.

The funeral of Mr. Johnson was attended by a numerous procession on Wednesday morning, the Rev. Mr. Watkins of the Methodist Church performing the religious services. This event has made a deep and painful impression upon our community.

The William Johnson House Museum

Baylor Winn was arrested for the murder, but in the trial his defense lawyer argued that he was actually white and not a free black man because of his Indian ancestry in Virginia. Since William Johnson was mulatto, the same designation passed to his son, who was prevented from testifying against Winn – Mississippi law of the day permitted blacks to testify against whites in civil cases, but not in criminal cases. After three trials, the juries were all undecided about the ethnic origins of the parties, and who could testify against whom, so William Johnson's murderer went free.

William Johnson's Grave in Natchez City Cemetery

This is not the end of the Barber of Natchez' legacy, however. His fourteen leather-bound volumes of diaries from 1835-1851 constitute one of the most important pieces of 19th century Natchez history in existence.

Today you can visit William's home where the plaster was

made with human hair from the barbershop. The bottom floor is now a museum administered by the National Parks Service to honor William and his diary, and the upper floor's rooms are preserved as they looked during his day – a photo of the building is at the start of this chapter. You can even purchase a copy of his diaries to read for yourself, and get a peek into the world of 1800s Natchez for a free black man. All-in-all, the diary of the Barber of Natchez is one of the most interesting historical documents of the city that we have today.

William Johnson House
210 State Street
Natchez, Mississippi 39120
601.445.5345

Melrose Plantation

The story of beautiful Melrose mansion is one of dreams and tragedy for the McMurran family. John McMurran was a successful Natchez attorney who married the beautiful Mary Louise Turner, the daughter of a prominent family. She had high aspirations for her husband, and even though he had been elected into the state legislature, Mary Louise wanted more for him. The problem was her husband – John was perfectly content to be a cotton plantation owner. Granted, he was successful in that regard, since he had five plantations, but there were many cotton kings in Natchez.

Mary Louise must have decided that she would be content to build a glorious mansion for the family. She approached her husband about her dream-home, but he was concerned that such an endeavor would be too much of a strain on their finances. She continued to mentally design their mansion, always sharing her latest thoughts with John. He eventually came around, however, and began to get excited about the project. Some say that he embraced it so passionately that he talked about it as if the entire thing was his idea to begin with.

One hundred thirty-three acres of land on the outskirts of town was purchased in 1841, and construction was begun. Slaves made the bricks on the site to be used in the mansion and its supporting buildings.

Their home, named Melrose, exceeded the couple's dreams. It featured a double-deck portico supported by large, Tuscan columns. It was built in the classic Greek revival style, with a double parlor for entertaining and a dining room with a mahogany "punkah," a large fan over the table.

The Dining Room, With The Punkah Over The Table

The family moved in at the very end of 1848, where they enjoyed life in their dream home for about fifteen years — the

113

Civil War that ravaged the country took its toll on Melrose. Not on the mansion itself; the family entertained some of the occupying Northern officers hoping to secure safety for Melrose. Instead, the devastation came after the war ended. Like many of the city's cotton kings, the McMurran family experienced financial setbacks in the carpetbagger economy; Melrose became too much of a burden. They were forced to sell the house in 1865, which sent both John and Mary Louise into a depression – their dream-home was gone. Melrose was sold to George Malin Davis, a friend of the McMurran family and an attorney in Natchez.

One of Melrose's Parlors

Sadly, the loss of Melrose was not to be the final tragedy for the McMurran family. After Christmas of 1866, John set out for New Orleans on the steamship *Fashion*. It carried not only three hundred passengers, but also 2,600 bales of cotton.

The ship stopped in ports along the way, but a few miles before it reached Baton Rouge, sparks from the chimney drifted down to the deck and ignited a bale of cotton. Mass panic and confusion erupted – smoke billowed to cloud every deck.

The pilot of the *Fashion* knew the river well, and felt that if they could make it around the next corner he would be able to land on shore there safely. But on board the situation worsened.

Everything seemed to be burning; horses that were being transported downriver bolted, leaping into the water and knocked over anything – and anyone – in their path. As the ship slowly steamed around the corner toward safety, the wind seemed to be working against them. It picked up and stoked the flames until the entire ship was engulfed. There were screams of pain and horror as passengers were burned alive; the fortunate ones were killed by inhalation of the billowing smoke.

The pilot finally saw the bank that he was looking for, and steered the steamship aground. The people who had fled to the fore end of the ship were able to jump to safety, but those on the aft end were trapped with the fire growing ever closer.

Some people that had jumped to shore saw that their families were trapped on the other end of the boat, and watched helplessly as they perished terribly. Some tried to swim to help, but the currents of the river pulled them underneath and they were drowned.

Soon the screams subsided; the night was filled only with the crackling of the fire and the sobbing of the survivors on the shore.

Both the pilot and the engineer stayed at their posts and were killed in the fire. John McMurran had been one of the fortunate ones who had been on the front of the ship. But when he attempted to jump off the ship, he broke his hip. John died in a New Orleans hospital a few days later.

Meanwhile, Melrose continued on. It remained in the

115

Davis family, passing first to George Malin Davis' daughter, and then to her son George Kelly. Twenty years went by with George Kelly and his wife owners in absentia – they lived in New York, and for two decades Melrose sat empty. A woman known only as "Aunt Jane" was its unofficial caretaker, making sure that no mischief befell the house.

In 1909 Mr. and Mrs. Kelly moved back to Natchez, and Aunt Jane helped them settle into Melrose and to shape the old mansion into their home. They repaired any problems, and brought the house back to its original beauty. Aunt Jane became a regular member of the family, helping them acclimate to Natchez life.

George Kelly passed away in 1945, leaving his wife to attend an ailing Aunt Jane. When Jane's friends came to visit her Mrs. Kelly was quick to caution them not to mention George's death – since Aunt Jane wasn't aware that it had happened, Mrs. Kelly did not want to upset her.

Melrose would change hands only twice more; John and Betty Callon purchased it in 1976, and then the National Parks Service acquired it in 1990. Today it is lovingly preserved by the Parks Service and is open to the public for tours; Melrose is shining example of antebellum Natchez.

Melrose Plantation
1 Melrose-Montebello Parkway
Natchez, MS 39120
601.446.5790

St. Mary's Basilica

There has been a Catholic presence in Natchez since about 1700 – a French Catholic parish was founded there in 1722. The Catholic Church in Natchez saw several international occupations of the city, and in 1788, a Spanish Catholic Church named San Salvador was established. The city joined the diocese of Louisiana in 1793; Catholics in the city kept their practices without a priest in residence until 1839.

The Diocese of Natchez, the center of the Catholic Church for the State of Mississippi, was established in 1837. Bishop John J. Chanche was the first officiating bishop.

Bishop Chanche wasted no time; he soon began construction on a cathedral in Natchez. Its cornerstone was laid on February 24, 1842 and the finished church was dedicated on Christmas, December 25, 1843 even though it was nowhere

117

near complete.

The church was finally finished in 1886, and the consecration ceremony was held on September 19, 1886. St. Mary's remained the Cathedral of the Diocese until 1977.

The Interior of St. Mary's Basilica

A cathedral is a church building presided over by a bishop, and therefore the central church building of a diocese, the administrative unit of the larger church. The word cathedral is actually shortened from the term "cathedral church." The term is used as an adjective in that case, because a cathedral is a church containing the cathedra – Latin for "chair" – of the bishop.

In the ancient world, the chair was a symbol of both a teacher and a magistrate, and therefore ideal for representing the power and duties of the bishop. What makes a cathedral a cathedral is the presence of the bishop, not anything inherent in the building itself. Therefore, a church building may gain or lose cathedral status, as St. Mary's did.

Twelve of its beautiful stained glass windows, by Tyroler Glassmalerie of Innsbruch, Germany, were installed between the years of 1884–1893, and four additional ones by Emil Frei of St Louis, Missouri, were installed in 1961.

The three marble altars, communion rail, Episcopal chair, and screens are fashioned from Carrara marble, carved in Italy in Gothic style for St. Mary, were all installed in 1930. The new altar of celebration and pulpit were installed in 1991.

The bell of St. Mary's was a gift from Price Alexander Torloni of Italy dated 1848; the work of Giovanni Lucenti of Italy. The bell was put into place on May 27, 1850, and its weight was a massive 3000 pounds. Torloni named it *Maria Alexandrina* in memory of his wife. The bell served St. Mary's until an automated bell system was installed by the Verdin Company in June 2002.

On September 8, 1998, St Mary was designated as a Minor Basilica and was formally dedicated as such on September 25, 1999. A complete exterior and interior renovation was completed June 2, 2002 and the church was once again open for tours by the public.

St. Mary Basilica
105 South Union St.
Natchez, MS 39121

The Yellow Jack in Natchez

There were two words that could bring terror in the heart of any man, woman or child in the city of Natchez during the mid-1800s. It wasn't the name of a river pirate or a Trace outlaw; it wasn't a dastardly riverboat captain, or any other sort of ruffian. No, it was simply "Yellow Jack," another name for the American Plague, the Black Vomit, or as it was more commonly known, Yellow Fever.

In Natchez, Yellow fever reached epidemic proportions in 1853. In *The Transactions of the American Medical Association*, published by the American Medical Association in 1854, the previous year's yellow fever plague in Natchez was described by a physician as follows: "At Natchez, on the Mississippi River, three hundred miles above New Orleans, the epidemic commenced about the middle of July, and prevailed with unprecedented violence for more than two months. Indeed, cases were seen there as late as December. This city has maintained a quarantine against yellow fever ever since 1841; yet I have been informed by some of the most respectable physicians of the place, that since that period scarcely a summer has passed without the appearance of some yellow fever cases there, either originating spontaneously, or brought from other places. I have tried in vain to obtain a history of the late epidemic at Natchez. The only thing I have seen on the subject was a letter from Dr. Luke P. Blackburn, physician to the Natchez Marine Hospital, in reply to interrogatories sent out by a committee of the Louisiana Legislature. To the question as to the origin of yellow fever, he replies, 'Yellow fever is undoubtedly of African, West Indian, or other tropical climates, generated in the hottest season of the year, and transmissible by its infectious and contagious qualities, to other places where it would never have originated.'

120

In reply to the question, 'Was the epidemic of last year contagious; and it was imported into New Orleans?' he says, 'I give decided and affirmative answers.'"

On August 31, 1853, the New York Times reported "Accounts from Natchez state that the greatest alarm was prevailing there, and more than half of the inhabitants had left the city in consequence of the ravages of the yellow fever. None of the authorities had left. Quarantine was no longer enforced."

It was truly a frightening time, and beginning about halfway through the year in 1853. A woman in New Orleans died of yellow fever, and people began to panic. Her father boarded a steamship several days later, getting off at Natchez because he was not feeling well. He soon died, and his death is considered to be the first victim of yellow fever in the city in 1853... but many more would follow.

At the time, no one knew how yellow fever spread, and so many speculative theories surfaced. One rumor spread that a postal worker had opened a contaminated package from New Orleans, infecting all the postal carriers who spread the disease through the city on their daily routes.

A more common belief was that it was in the soil – that it was spread when the Earth was disturbed. In his book, *Yellow Fever Considered In Its Historical, Pathological, Etiological, And Therapeutical Relations*, R. LaRouche says, "Now, that these experiments did render Natchez sickly, there can be no reason to doubt. The coincidences were too striking to be viewed as accidental. Besides, the same effects following the same causes have been observed elsewhere." He goes on to quote Dr. E.H. Barton, of New Orleans, who said, "...to whose report on the sanitary condition of that city in 1853 reference has been made on several occasions, and who has borrowed the above facts, states, on good authority, that again, notwithstanding previous warnings, in 1853, at Natchez, the leveling of the streets by the cutting down the adjoining banks, and superposing the fresh earth on the streets, resulted in the fever. It is said to have first broken out in the immediate neighbourhood where this took place – that here occurred its largest mortality, and thence it spread to the neighbourhood."

Basically, the yellow fever was blamed on the stirring of dirt in the city. It was truly a terrible disease – its name came from the fact that the afflicted became quite jaundiced, or yellow. The condition is preceded by fever, chills, and head and back pain. Nausea, vomiting, and constipation are common, and the substance vomited is a combination of blood and bile that has a blackish color.

From there it was a nightmarish descent for those who had been infected. Delirium and coma followed, and death became a welcome relief.

One physician in Natchez, a Dr. Davis, said that the population of the city before the epidemic numbered about 6,500 – but dropped to 3,500 because of the disease. Hundreds died a terrible death brought by Yellow Fever; many gathered their family and possessions, and fled the city to escape the disease.

It is said that grass grew in the city streets during that time because those who did stay closed themselves inside their homes. Businesses were closed, and the normal operation of the city came to a halt.

Slowly, the number of cases began to decline, and life in Natchez returned to normal – or as normal as it could be in the wake of an epidemic of such deadly proportions.

Not that the city let down their guard; anyone showing the slightest signs of the disease was quarantined, and folks still raised a worried eyebrow when the dirt was turned over for new buildings or street work. No one knew for sure how Yellow Fever spread, and there was always a little nervousness that it would return to the city on the bluff.

One interesting story came out of the fear of Yellow Jack, however. Doctor Luke Blackburn, a doctor and philanthropist quoted earlier in the chapter, took a novel approach to fighting against the North during the Civil War. He sought out people who had the disease, and took their clothing and bedding. Since it was still not known how Yellow Fever was spread, he assumed that the "infected" items carried the disease.

He packed the items in trunks, and shipped them to Northern cities hoping to start epidemics there that would hopefully cripple the Union. His plan didn't work, although interestingly enough it was one of the first attempts at biological warfare in the U.S.

Eventually it was discovered that Yellow Jack was spread by ordinary mosquitoes. By the turn of the century a vaccine had been developed that tamed the disease that was once the scourge of the South.

Dunleith

The story of Dunleith begins back during the Spanish period of Natchez' history, in the late 1700s, when a young man named Job Routh married Ann Miller, who was a sister of the Spanish Government's Secretary of State.

Job obtained a 1700-acre land grant from the government, and set out to build a fine mansion for his bride. When it was completed, the home was stocked with European furnishings and became one of the showplaces of Natchez; it was known as "Routhland." As each of the Routh children grew up and married, they were given a piece of the original land grant, where they each built grand houses of their own. As a cotton baron, Job Routh became one of the wealthiest men in Natchez – he owned much land and many slaves.

Job and Ann's daughter Mary was widowed at the young age of fifteen, and after marrying her second husband, Charles

124

G. Dahlgren, inherited Routhland upon the death of her parents.

Dahlgren was a direct descendant of Sweden's King Gustavus Adolphus, and the son of the first Swedish Consul to the United States. The couple made their home there, and Mary insisted on adorning the mansion with terra-cotta chimneys. In the mid-1800s, tragedy struck while they were vacationing up North. Lightening struck the house during a thunderstorm, and Routhland burned to the ground. Charles Dahlgren always blamed Mary's chimneys for the disaster.

The Dahlgrens completed construction of the house that stands on the property today in 1856. The elegant home featured 26 columns that completely surrounded the house, making it the only dwelling in Mississippi with such a colonnade.

Tragedy struck at the property again, however, when Mary died in 1859, only three years after their new home had been completed. Her husband was forced to sell the house because of estate issues, and it passed to Alfred Vidal Davis, who purchased it for the princely sum of $30,000.

Mr. Davis was among the richest cotton planters in Louisiana, and a descendant of Don José Vidal, for whom the town of Vidalia, Louisiana is named. At that time, his land produced over three thousand bales of cotton and seventeen thousand bushels of corn.

Davis is credited with changing the name of the house from "Routhland" to "Dunleith." Mr. Davis was known for his love of champagne, and he commissioned a special glass to be made for his parties – it was shaped like a horn, with the flat open mouth of the vessel tapering down to a pointed bottom.

Because of its shape, the glass could never be put down on the table, and therefore his guests would always have a drink in hand.

Dunleith was purchased in 1886 by another man who had made his fortune in cotton, Joseph Carpenter. His family occupied Dunleith for five generations, having someone in residence there for almost one hundred years.

One Of Dunleith's Inviting Galleries

In 1976 the mansion was sold to William F. Heins, who opened the doors to the public for the first time, running Dunleith as a bed and breakfast inn for over twenty years. The Worley Companies purchased Dunleith in 1999, and Mrs. Edward Worley and her son Michael Worley began a restoration of the mansion, giving it the love, care, and attention that it needed.

Today, visitors can enjoy the beauty and serenity of Dunleith, along with its many other amenities.

Behind the house is the Castle Restaurant & Pub, featuring delightful cuisine in the restored 1790s Carriage House. You'll enjoy grilled duck breast, pork tenderloin, rib eye steak, and many other tempting items to round out your stay at Dunleith.

The Castle Restaurant & Pub

Dunleith Historic Inn
84 Homochitto St
Natchez, MS 39120
601.446.8500
www.dunleith.com

Rosswood Plantation

A little north of Natchez, just off of the Trace, is an 1857 plantation home that is simply a delight to visit. The 1250-acre plantation was originally purchased by Dr. Walter Ross Wade in 1848 from the estate of his grandfather Captain Issac Ross; he paid $5000.00, which was $4.00 per acre. Wade called the cotton plantation "Rosswood" in honor of his grandfather.

Architect David Schroeder was commissioned to build a mansion there for Wade and his wife-to-be Mabella Chamberlain; he contracted for a $10,000 lump-sum payment. As with any construction project there were overruns, and the extra charges of $2,850 made Dr. Wade angry.

There were problems encountered during the construction – the brickwork, for example. The entire house was supposed to be made of brick, manufactured on the property by slave labor. The brick started crumbling, and the builder was forced to search for a way to make better-quality brick. This took too much time, so Dr. Wade said, "Just go ahead and make it a frame house, so that I can get married!"

The mansion was built in the classic Greek Revival architectural style, consisting of 14 rooms and 14-foot ceilings. It has 10 fireplaces throughout the house, a winding stairway, and the original slave quarters.

During his life there, Dr. Wade, kept a journal describing his courtship and marriage of Mabella, and their plantation life before and during the Civil War. It consists of three volumes covering the years 1834 to 1862. Volumes 1 and 2 are basically ledgers, but Volume 3 is his candid and sometimes humorous narrative of plantation life.

In this journal, the good doctor describes the construction of the Rosswood mansion; parties, balls, and other social events; a slave revolt; and management of the cotton plantation. The diaries also document the story about how Wade's grandfather, Issac Ross, freed his slaves and paid for their return to Africa, in direct violation of a state law banning emancipation of slaves.

Rosswood plantation thrived under the ownership of Dr. Wade, and at its peak there were 105 slaves working the fields. The doctor died of melanoma on July 12th, 1862, at age 52, leaving his wife Maybella as a 42-year-old widow with eight children and a plantation to run.

The Civil War was in full swing by then, and it appeared that Northern forces would soon make their way to Mississippi. Maybella was worried that the treasures of Rosswood would be pillaged, so she put all of the family silver and jewelry into a locked chest, and told two slaves to take it out and bury it on the plantation to protect it from any invading troops that might pass by.

As it turned out, the war did come to Rosswood, in the "Battle of the Cotton Bales." On March 15, 1864 as the Civil War was starting to wind down, a contingent of Union soldiers stationed on the Mississippi were told by their scouts of a warehouse filled with cotton bales just a few miles to the east.

Since the northern mills were greatly in need of cotton, they marched out to seize the prize; unfortunately, their scouts had miscalculated the Confederate Army presence in the area. The Union troops were ambushed just east of what is now Highway 61 and the Southern soldiers soon fought them back to the river.

Four months later the Yankees tried to capture the warehouse once again. By then, the Confederate forces had tripled in size, so the skirmish once again went to the South. In this second assault, the Union army brought one piece of artillery, and in the shelling during the battle the stand-alone kitchen of Rosswood was hit by a shell. The current owner, Walt Hylander, found a piece of the shell; it is on display in the house.

Wounded from both sides were taken to Rosswood during the battle, which served as a makeshift hospital. One Union soldier died in a bedroom from the wounds sustained in the skirmish, and was buried in the family cemetery.

Word was sent to his family in Indiana that he had been given a Christian burial, but after the war was over his family came down to retrieve the body and take it back home.

Once the war was over Maybella discovered that her plan to save the family treasures had worked well, but she was reluctant to dig up the locked chest because she knew that it would be heavily taxed by the carpetbaggers in public office at the time.

Instead, she decided to wait until the storm of the post-Civil War era had passed. Time went by; the slaves who buried the chest died, as did Mrs. Wade, and the secret location of the chest was lost with them.

There may be a few ghosts in residence at Rosswood, but if that is the case, they are certainly friendly spirits. One story was recorded by Annie (Clark) Jacobs, the daughter of Charles

Clark (Brigadier General, C.S.A., Governor of Mississippi, 1863-1865) and Anne Eliza (Darden) Clark. She had stayed at Rosswood at the age of twelve, and gave the following account: *"When I heard the latch of the hall door and looked up to see the door closing, I though, 'How funny,' for I knew the door had been closed. However, I read on in my book. The door opened again and again, but when I looked up it closed. I thought this was a foolish fancy of mine and at the sound of the latch and the opening of the door for the third time, I did not look up. The door opened and the sound of light feet on the matting and the sound like a silk dress rustling at each step, entered. I was spellbound, afraid to look. I heard light footsteps and this dress brushed by the bed and passed on to the window. It seemed to go out of the window and I looked again – there was nothing. There was no gallery outside and the blinds were closed to all four of the French windows. I heard the steps and the rustling dress again – a reassuring thought that it was just the wind blowing, but it was in the room again, coming nearer to me. At each window it faded away and returned. I had a tallow candle on the arm of an old fashioned reading chair. I was scared to death, afraid to look, afraid to scream. This sound now came tripping across the marble hearth. It came nearer, the light went out and I knew no more until I felt myself dashed with cold water and the family around me. I was asked to say nothing about this and told that only the blood kin of the Ross family ever had these ghostly experiences, but oh, the tales that Pauline and her brother Duncan told me afterwards."*

When you visit Rosswood today, you will see many reminders of its past. Dr. Wade's diaries are on display there, and you can see the cannonball that hit the kitchen during the Battle of the Cotton Bales. You should also bring a shovel along, because to this day no one has found the family treasure that is still buried somewhere on the property.

Colonel Walt Hylander and his wife Jean have owned

131

Rosswood since 1975, and they are consummate hosts. The plantation today has one hundred acres surrounding the house, populated by wildlife for you to enjoy. It is still a working plantation, but instead of cotton it now produces Christmas trees.

The Parlor At Rosswood

Rosswood is a registered Mississippi Landmark, and is listed on the National Register of Historic Places for history and architecture. The plantation has been shown on the Travel Channel, and is called "The Prettiest Place in the Country."

Rosswood Plantation
2513 Red Lick Road
Lorman, MS 39096
800.533.5889
www.rosswood.net

Stanton Hall

The War of 1812 lasted for about four years, fought between America on one side and England, Ireland and other British colonies on the other. Following the war, life in the country of Ireland was characterized by poor harvests and depressed markets – times were tough on the Emerald Isle.

A young man named Frederick Stanton immigrated to America from Belfast, Ireland, in 1815 at the end of the war. At twenty-one years of age, he used his negotiation skills to become a cotton broker in the city of Natchez, and after establishing himself as a successful businessman, married Hulda Laura Helm.

Mr. Stanton's fortunes grew over the next decade, and construction was started on a palatial mansion home in downtown Natchez. By then he owned 444 slaves and 16,000 acres of land in all of his holdings; he was literally one of the

133

richest men in the county.

Stanton's home would occupy an entire city block, and as the story goes, a ship was chartered to bring items for the house from Europe that included the mantles, ironwork, moldings, and furnishings. Stanton made inquiries around town about the most skilled craftsmen to build the house, and he negotiated for their services. Many were slaves whose masters hired their services out in the manner like any contractor might do today, and their talents were highly prized in Natchez.

In 1857 Frederick Stanton's mansion was complete. With its magnificent Corinthian columns, the house had a total of 14,000 square feet, over a thousand of which was in the entry hallway alone. It was a showplace in a city populated by showplaces. Huge mirrors and mantles adorned every room; front and back parlors on the first floor joined to form a huge room for entertaining.

Tragedy struck in 1859, only two years after the house was completed: Frederick Stanton contracted yellow fever and died on January 4th of that year. His family continued to live in the house for the next thirty-four years, until his wife's death on September 2nd, 1893.

During the Union occupation of Natchez in the Civil War, Union Army flags were raised at Stanton Hall, which may have helped protect it from the invading forces.

The mansion became a boarding college for young women after Mrs. Stanton's death, and eventually it was purchased by the Pilgrimage Garden Club in 1938.

Not only is the house on tour throughout the year, but it also serves as a part of the Spring and Fall Pilgrimages in Natchez. Today, Stanton Hall has been restored as it might have looked in the 1850s when it was constructed. It features many furnishings that have been returned to the house by descendents who have inherited the pieces and wanted them to return home. The house was designated as a National Historic Landmark in 1974.

Stanton Hall's Gardens

The gardens on the property date from 1851, and feature live oak trees, azaleas, camellias, daylilies, caladiums and other beautiful plants.

Behind Stanton Hall you will find the southern-cooking Carriage House Restaurant, featuring buttered biscuits, mint juleps, southern fried chicken, and tomato aspic. It is a popular place to dine for locals as well as visitors to the town.

Stanton Hall
401 High Street
Natchez, Mississippi 39120
601.442.6282
www.StantonHall.com

135

Magnolia Hall

Magnificent Magnolia Hall was built in 1858 by a gentleman named Thomas Henderson. He was a merchant, planter, and held the office of elder in the First Presbyterian Church of Natchez. Henderson had been elected vice-president of the American Colonization Society in 1853. It was an organization formed to free slaves, and then return them to Africa. Mr. Henderson had a long and distinguished record of civic service.

He was sixty years old and a widower when he started construction of Magnolia Hall. Thomas came from a prominent pioneer family – his father, John Henderson, came to America from Scotland in 1770. John owned several plantations in the Natchez countryside, and authored the first book published in the territory. John was also one of the founders of the First Presbyterian Church in 1807, which is probably one of the

136

reasons that it was so dear to Thomas' heart.

The house was built on the site of his family home, Pleasant Hill. The original house was so beautiful that he didn't want to have it torn down. Instead, it was raised, put on log rollers, and moved one block away where it still sits today.

Henderson's home features an immense portico with large upper and lower galleries on both the front and rear elevations of the house. Inside of the home, magnolia-and-leaf ceiling medallions are the feature that gives the house its name. There are six rooms on the main floor, and six additional rooms on the second floor.

Brownstone was very popular in the northeastern United States at the time the house was built, so Thomas Henderson had his house stuccoed, painted brown, and scored to mimic the distinctive look. No one knew it at the time, but Magnolia Hall would be the last great mansion built in the city of Natchez before the Civil War.

When the War Between the States erupted, Thomas Henderson's two sons each fought for the Confederacy. One of them was wounded, the other taken prisoner.

During the war, there was only one incident when Natchez was under attack. That was in 1862 when Captain W.D. Porter, Commander of the gunboat Essex, briefly shelled the city in response to an attack on his soldiers by the citizens during a brief stopover. A shell from the ship struck the service wing of Magnolia Hall, landing in the soup tureen. Although no one was injured, it gave the house distinctive bragging rights – it was one of the few houses in Natchez shelled by the Union troops, and it survived to tell the tale.

In 1863 Thomas Henderson suffered a paralytic stroke, and since it became impossible for him to go up the stairs to his bedroom he took up residence in the guest bedroom downstairs. Confined to the bed, he died on March 6, 1863 from a cerebral hemorrhage. His body was removed from the house and interred at the Natchez City Cemetery. An inventory of the house's furnishings was made upon his death, to aid in the settlement of his estate, providing an exact listing of what Magnolia Hall contained at the time.

A Magnolia Hall Parlor

Shortly thereafter, the house was sold to the Britton family, who occupied it for many years. Following that, it became a boarding house, then a private Episcopal School. During the Episcopal years, all of the original partitioned walls were taken out to facilitate classrooms, and all but two of the original mantelpieces were sold. The ceilings of the beautiful old home were lowered, probably to aid in the heating and cooling of the classrooms for the students. The original chandeliers were sold, and Magnolia Hall took on a much more institutional appearance.

It continued to change owners, but the house was re-born in 1976, when it was deeded to the Natchez Garden Club by

Mrs. George Armstrong of Fort Worth, Texas. A full restoration was undertaken under the supervision of the New Orleans architectural firm Koch and Wilson, with the assistance of the Mississippi Department of Archives and History. Over the years since they have owned it, the club has acquired many of the original Henderson furnishings.

Upstairs where there were once plush bedrooms, you will now find a costume museum including many gowns of Natchez Pilgrimage Queens. Photographs of the city's Pilgrimage royalty are also displayed; the upper floor is a tribute to the pageantry that is such a major part of the city of Natchez.

The Pilgrimage Costume Museum Upstairs

Today, Magnolia Hall is the site of luncheons and candlelight dinners served by the Natchez Garden Club members for visitors to the city all year. The house is listed on the National Register of Historic Places, and is open for tours.

Magnolia Hall
215 South Pearl Street
Natchez, MS 39120
601.442.6847
www.natchezgardenclub.com/mag.htm

Longwood

As any visitor knows – or soon discovers – Natchez is a city filled with stately Antebellum mansions. Each has a particular beauty and its own distinctive features, but there is one in particular that is so dramatically different that it requires a second or even third glance. It is called Longwood, and it is perhaps one of the most unique homes in the South.

Conceived as a "town house" for Haller and Julia Nutt, the octagonal brick house with the onion-shaped dome was designed by prominent Philadelphia architect Samuel Sloan in 1859. Mr. Nutt was so taken by the images of the house that he began to brag that, "...after Longwood, everyone would be building an octagonal home."

It was to be a mansion to befit Nutt's status as a wealthy planter and businessman. There would be three stories and a basement, a rotunda looking up into the massive dome, and

141

thirty-two rooms.

Beginning in 1860, Cypress trees were felled and cut for the house, a brick manufacturing site with a kiln was established, builders and craftsmen were hired from as far north as Pennsylvania and construction on the house began in earnest.

The threat of a War Between the States had been looming on the horizon and the hostilities were brought to a reality in 1861. Longwood's exterior was near completion, but the workers from the North laid down their tools and quickly headed for home, leaving the interior of the house completely unfinished.

Looking Up Into Longwood's Rotunda

Haller Nutt used his slaves and local craftsmen to complete the basement floor and make it livable for the duration of the war. He did not agree with Mississippi's decision to secede from the Union, and publicly opposed the Confederacy.

His dedication to the United States did not save his holdings, however. His Louisiana plantation of some 40,000 acres was destroyed by Union Troops, along with most buildings there. The cotton that had been baled was appropriated by the Confederates – it seems that both sides took a piece of Mr. Nutt.

His fortune had been decimated, and he was a ruined man living in an unfinished mansion. Few people were sympathetic; they began to call Longwood "Nutt's folly."

Longwood's Ornate Exterior

Stress and worry took their toll on Nutt; and in 1864 he contracted pneumonia. He died on June 16th. His wife, Julia, blamed his death on the Union army, and she continued to live in the basement floor with their children.

When the war was over, Julia demanded reparations from

the government of the United States, requesting a sum of three million dollars to cover the family's losses. When listing the assets that were lost, she reportedly listed her husband: "Life of Haller Nutt; value: HOW MUCH?"

The case went all the way to the Supreme Court, who heard it on April 2, 1888. Among the evidence heard, the records state, "...that the Quartermaster General of the United States is hereby authorized to examine and adjust the claims of Julia A. Nutt, widow and executrix of Haller Nutt, deceased, late of Natchez, in the State of Mississippi, growing out of the occupation and use by the United States Army during the late rebellion of the property of said Haller Nutt during his lifetime, or of his estate after his decease, including livestock, goods, and moneys, taken and used by the United States or the armies thereof, and he may consider the evidence heretofore taken on said claim, as far as applicable, before the Commissioners of Claims, and such other evidence as may be adduced before him on behalf of the legal representatives of Haller Nutt or on behalf of the United States, and shall report the facts to Congress to be considered with other claims reported by the Quartermaster General."

The Quartermaster General reported a total amount of $256,884.05 as the total Nutt family loss, but payment was not acted upon. On July 5, 1884, Congress passed an act to pay some reparations for the war, of which part reads: "To Julia A. Nutt, widow and executrix of Haller Nutt, deceased, of Adams County, the sum of $35,556.17."

Julia accepted the amount, probably grudgingly, but the family needed money. She continued to seek more, but the United States Supreme Court declared that the matter had been duly settled.

Julia continued to raise the family's eight children in the nine-room basement of Longwood, which Haller Nutt had finished out with the grandeur of any proper mansion. Her family, although sometimes struggling, were raised to be proper and educated. Mrs. Julia Nutt passed away on February 23rd, 1897.

Today, visitors to Natchez can tour the mansion that hasn't changed much through the years. It is operated by the Pilgrimage Garden Club, who is now the caretaker of Nutt's dream. The downstairs retains all the elegance that it had when the Nutt family lived there, while the upstairs remains as unfinished as when the workers laid down their tools and walked away – it stands as monument to the hopes and dreams that were dashed by the devastating Civil War.

Longwood
140 Lower Woodville Road
Natchez MS, 39120
601.442.5193

The Windsor Ruins

Just a short drive from Natchez are the ruins of what must have been a breathtaking mansion. It's not that hard to find, especially if you're following the Natchez Trace – just look for the *Windsor Ruins* signs. When you arrive, you'll see that there is something very foreboding about the place. It just feels, well, ee*rie*.

Walk beside the massive columns and you'll see that the air seems very still, and there is an unsettling quietness around the ruins. I think that it is because you are basically looking at the skeleton of a house. When you look at it, you see the "bones" that are left, but your mind races with the majesty of how it must have once looked.

The Windsor plantation once covered over 2,600 acres, and the house was built around 1860 by Smith Coffee Daniell II. Unfortunately, Daniell died only a few weeks after it was

146

completed. It cost $175,000 – not a small amount in those days – which included the construction and all of its furnishings. The mansion contained twenty-five rooms, with twenty-five fireplaces, and twenty-nine forty-five-foot-high Corinthian columns with steel caps and wrought iron balusters flanked the building. The first floor contained a dairy, schoolroom, and several storage rooms.

Four sets of iron steps led from the ground to the second floor, which was the main floor of the house. Twelve-foot wide verandas swept around the house, providing what must have been a wonderful place to relax and enjoy the view.

Most of the rooms in the house were nineteen by twenty feet, with 16-foot ceilings.

A Sketch Of Windsor

There were several efficiencies built in as well, including tanks in the attic that supplied water for the interior bathrooms on the second and third floors.

The only known likeness of the Windsor Mansion is from a drawing made by Henry Otis Dwight, who was a first lieutenant with the 20th Ohio Infantry. It was found in his diary, and was probably made when his unit camped on the grounds of Windsor Mansion before fighting in the Battle of Port Gibson on May 1, 1863.

Basic construction of the house was designed by David Shroder and was built by slave labor. Mr. Shroder also designed and built Rosswood Plantation – see its chapter elsewhere in this book. The bricks that were used in the 45-foot columns were made in a kiln across the road from the house. The columns were then covered with mortar and plaster.

To finish the house, skilled carpenters were brought in from New England for the finished woodwork and the iron stairs. Column capitals and balustrades were manufactured in St. Louis and shipped down the Mississippi River to the Port of Bruinsburg several miles west of Windsor.

There is much legend and lore concerning Windsor:

- Windsor narrowly escaped destruction during the Civil War when Ulysses S. Grant's troops mistakenly fired on the veranda chairs assuming they were Confederate soldiers.
- Confederate forces used the roof observatory as an look-out platform and signal station before the house was occupied by Union troops.
- A Yankee soldier was shot in the front doorway.
- The mansion was used as a Union hospital and observation post during the Civil War, which is why it was not burned by the northern troops at the time.
- Mark Twain was a guest at the house, and while traveling the river, would point at it and tell fellow travelers that it was a college instead of a house, due to its size.

No matter which of those things are true, there is one sad certainty: the house burned during a house party on February 17, 1890. Some say that a guest left a lighted cigar on the upper balcony. Another story has the guest tossing a lit cigarette into a trashcan that happened to be full of paper. There are other theories as well, but however the fire started, one thing is certain: Windsor would have fared much better had they instituted a "no smoking" policy.

After the place had been reduced to embers, only the pillars and the wrought iron staircase remained. You can see the pillars at the ruins, of course, and one set of stairs is now a part of nearby Alcorn State University.

The Windsor Ruins have appeared in several Hollywood films, including *Raintree County* (1957), starring Elizabeth Taylor, Montgomery Cliff, Lee Marvin, Eva Marie Saint, and DeForest Kelley. The columns also appeared in the movie *Ghosts of Mississippi*. The following floor plan is based on a sketch made by Smith Coffee Daniell IV who drew it from memory and measurements made of the ruins. The exact plans were lost to the fire, but we are fortunate to have this recollection of what the house looked like.

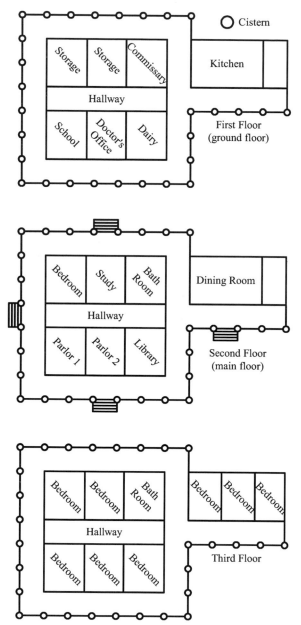

Smith C. Daniell IV's Floor Plan of the Windsor Mansion

When entering the house, a visitor would have climbed steps to the main floor, which was actually the second floor of the house. Missing from the floor plan is the fourth floor, which was a ballroom and observation room that was never completed. It was topped with a large cupola lined with gold, and local legend says that Confederate troops were signaled of Yankee advances from that cupola.

The fact that this beautiful home burned to the ground is a tragedy indeed. The family said the fire started around 3:00 in the afternoon. A seated dinner had been planned for later, and the family had gone into town to pick up the mail. Riding back, they saw flames shooting through the shingled roof. The fire burned from top to bottom making it impossible to extinguish. Although the house was destroyed, we still have the columns of Windsor to reimind us of this beautiful plantation home.

Natchez in the Civil War

As Southern states were starting to secede from the Union to join the Confederacy, Mississippi held a statewide convention in 1859 where a resolution was adopted to split from the Union if the newly elected U.S. President was someone who opposed slavery. Abraham Lincoln won the office, of course, and Mississippi seceded on January 9, 1861. The next day, the Vicksburg Evening Citizen newspaper declared, "Mississippi is Out! Hereafter we must look upon the United States as a foreign country."

Within the next month, a total of seven states had declared their intention to part from the Union, and on February 9, 1861, each of these states sent delegates to meet in Montgomery, Alabama. This came to be known as the Confederate Congress, and the representatives there elected Jefferson Davis as the president of the Confederacy. Two days later President Davis gave a speech, saying, "...our safety and honor required us to dissolve our connection with the United States. I hope that our separation may be peaceful. But whether it be so or not, I am ready, as I have always been, to redeem my pledges to you and the South by shedding every drop of blood in your cause."

As the war escalated, the Mississippi River became increasingly important to the South – it was a lifeline for moving Confederate supplies and troops. Because of that, it was only a matter of time before the Northern forces began to focus their attention on the mighty river. The Union ships first focused on the Crescent City, and after New Orleans fell in April of 1862, it spurred the sudden evacuation of people up and down the river, all fearing the Northern forces. Merchants boarded up their stores, and the citizens left en masse.

Natchez' physical involvement in the war occurred during the month of May 1862, when Flag-Officer David G. Farragut led a flotilla of ships up the Mississippi toward the city of Natchez. He had participated in the battle of New Orleans and was ordered to secure ports further north for the Union. Part of his fleet included the U.S.S. Iroquois, commanded by James S. Palmer.

On May 12, 1862, the Union ships were anchored beside the city of Natchez and commander Palmer issued a dispatch to the city's mayor:

United States Steamer Iroquois, at Anchor Off Natchez, Miss., May 12, 1862.
To His Honor, the Mayor of Natchez.
Sir: In advance of the squadron now coming up the Mississippi, I am instructed by the Flag-Officer to demand the surrender of the City of Natchez to the naval forces of the United States.
The same terms will be accorded as those granted to New Orleans and Baton Rouge. The rights and property of all peaceable citizens shall be respected; but all property in the city belonging to the so-called Confederate States must be delivered up, and the flag of the United States must wave unmolested and respected over your town.
Very respectfully, your obedient servant,
Jas. S. Palmer, Commander.

The Mayor and Selectmen of the City of Natchez had assembled in a special meeting at 8 AM to discuss the demand. In attendance were: Mayor John Hunter, the City Clerk C.F. Merrick and the selectmen of the city – Mr. Baidwin, Mr. Curry, Mr. Dix, Mr. Walworth and Mr. Walker. After discussing the matter, Mayor Hunter was directed to make the following reply to Commander Palmer:

153

Mayor's Office, Natchez, Mississippi
May 13, 1862
To Jas. S. Palmer, Commander U.S.S. Iroquois, at anchor off
Natchez, Miss.
Sir:

Your communication of the 12th inst. has been received by me and laid before the Board of Selectmen of this City, and I am directed to return the following reply:

Coming as a conqueror, you need not the interposition of the city authorities to possess this place. An unfortified city, an entirely defenseless people, have no alternative but to yield to an irresistible force, as useless to imperil innocent blood. Formalities are absurd in the face of such realities.

So far as the city authorities can prevent, there will be no opposition to your possession of the city; they cannot, however, guarantee that your flag shall wave unmolested in the sight of an excited people; but such authority as they possess shall be exercised for the preservation of good order in the city.

As to property belonging to the Confederate States, they are not aware of any such within the limits of the city. Very respectfully, your obedient servant,
John Hunter, Mayor

Union forces under General Walter Gresham soon occupied the city, setting up headquarters in Rosalie Mansion. During this time, General Ulysses S. Grant visited Rosalie. For several months, the city led a peaceful existence during the War Between the States... until the month of September, 1862.

Captain W.D. Porter, Commander of the gunboat Essex, had received word that Confederate transport boats loaded with supplies such as cattle, salt and cotton had made for Natchez. Not to let the Southern forces run the river on his watch, he launched out in pursuit, and anchored on the river beside the city. The Essex was running low on fuel, so the commander ordered that the vessel take on coal from the town of Vidalia, which was directly across the river from Natchez. The Mayor of Vidalia protested this seizure of fuel, but the Union army confiscated the coal anyway.

The coaling was complete by 2 PM, but before leaving the area, Captain Porter moved across the river to Natchez to get ice for his sick and wounded men. As the sailors from the Essex were making their way back to the ship with the ice, they were suddenly attacked by two hundred armed citizens. One of the seamen was killed instantly, while another half-dozen were wounded. The crewmen made their way back to the ship. Upon learning of the attack, the Essex opened fire on the city of Natchez.

As the gunboat shelled the city, a volley of musket-fire swept the decks of the ship. The Essex left some degree of damage to Natchez. Fires broke out where the shells had landed, a cannonball landed in the kitchen of Magnolia Hall, and as a family was fleeing the barrage up Silver Street, a seven-year-old daughter of a Jewish family – Rosalie Beekman – was killed by a shell. Reportedly she uttered the words, "Papa, I am killed," as she died. Rosalie was the only casualty of the Civil War in Natchez. When the attacks from the city seemed to be subdued, Porter continued upriver toward Vicksburg.

Harper's Weekly gave the following account of the incident in the October 4, 1862 issue

The gunboat Essex, Commodore Porter, has made another expedition up the river. On reaching Natchez, the Essex sent a boat's crew ashore for ice. This lot was fired upon and several men were wounded, whereupon Commodore Porter threw shot and shell into Natchez for two hours and a half, when the town surrendered. Coming down the river, the Commodore stopped at Bayou Sara, a celebrated haunt of guerrillas, sent men ashore, and burned all but two houses—so there's an end of Bayou Sara. Further down the river, a battery of 34 guns opened on the Essex, and a fierce battle, at not more

155

than 80 feet distance, began, which lasted an hour. The rebel battery was mounted with guns of very heavy caliber; but that circumstance only sufficed to prove the remarkable powers of resistance of the Essex. Her iron sides were struck in a multitude of places with 10-inch and other sized balls, the result in all cases being the same—a slight indentation into the sides of the steamer, and then the balls breaking into a thousand fragments and falling harmlessly into the water. The Essex commenced with the upper gun and silenced them all, one after the other.

Later that year, forces from the Confederate army approached Natchez in December 1863 to try to re-take the town, but the sheer number of the Union forces that were present there made them turn back. There were many Natchez citizens, however, that remained loyal to the Confederacy. In 1864, the Roman Catholic bishop of the Diocese of Natchez, William Henry Elder, was given an order to pray for the President of the United States, and to instruct his parishioners to do so as well. When he refused, the Union army officials arrested the Bishop. They quickly tried and convicted him, jailing him briefly in the town of Vidalia, Louisiana, across the Mississippi River. Elder was eventually released and restored to his duties.

While other Southern cities never recovered from the ravages of the war, Natchez recovered quite quickly. The Mississippi River traffic recharged the city's economy – farming and industry flourished.

In the final tally of the Civil War, the city of Natchez contributed about 1,500 men, which constituted more than half of the town's white male population, to the Confederate cause. Three hundred of these men sacrificed their lives in the war. The Natchez City Cemetery is the final resting place for many of them, including four generals of the Southern Army.

The Great Riverboat Race

On June 30, 1870, one of the most dramatic and anticipated races in the history of our country took place on the Mississippi River – at the time it captured the heart and imagination of the country much as the Indianapolis 500 or the Kentucky Derby does today. It was a battle of the giants between the steamboat *Natchez*, captained by Thomas P. Leathers, and the *Robert E. Lee*, captained by John W. Cannon.

By that time, steamboats had already become the preferred method of travel on the river. They were opulent, catering to every whim of their travelers. The first such boat arrived in Natchez in 1811 – Captain Nicholas Roosevelt's *New Orleans*. More and more steamboats began to operate on the Mississippi, each trying to out-do the last. They managed to weather the storm of the Civil War, and seemed to be unwavering in their importance to the travel and shipping industries.

The ships were all of a very similar design; several stories of passenger decks with a wheelhouse on top. A huge paddlewheel provided the locomotion for moving along the river, and the wheel itself was often several stories high, with two smokestacks, each topped with an elaborate crown.

The insides of the steamboats boasted carpeting, chandeliers, statuary and furniture that could have graced any home in the South. The staterooms rivaled those of the grandest hotels; services to travelers included barber and beauty shops, saloons, dining rooms, gambling halls and anything else that a traveler might desire.

Over the years, many steamboats came and went. They were unfortunately susceptible to the dangers of the river. Some sank, others ran aground on sandbars. Stoking the fire to the boiler sometimes caught the vessels ablaze and the truly unfortunate ones simply exploded – both of these events were most common in steamboat races, a popular sport that sprang up in bids among the captains for superiority on the river. But none would capture the attention of the world like the contest between the *Natchez* and the *Robert E. Lee*.

Captain Leathers of the steamboat *Natchez* called the ship's namesake his home. He was a giant of a man, six-foot four inches tall, weighing two hundred sixty pounds. His hair, beard and mustache were all snow-white, providing a bright contrast to the ever-present cigar clinched between his teeth.

The Captain's presence was commanding, not just because of his stature, but also because of his boisterous spirit – some people revered him as the most talented curser on the river. In only a moment, he could switch from verbally assaulting a deckhand to complementing a passing lady with the finesse of a Natchez gentleman. Legend has it that he once sincerely told a friend, "What is the use of being a steamboat captain if you can't tell the entire world to go to hell?"

But for all his rough exterior, his generosity seemed to match his size. Stories were often told in Natchez of his willingness to help widows and children, or others in town who were down on their luck. He did so not for recognition, but out of genuine concern.

On the river, however, Leathers was a wild man. He would crowd other steamboats simply to intimidate their captains. If leaving port at the same time as another ship, he would delay his own departure just for the opportunity to overtake them.

The captain knew every trick in the book for passing on the river, from throwing a bucket of lard onto the fire for a sudden burst of energy, to cutting across the path of another boat on a river bend. Leathers had even been known to fire a cannon across the bow of other boats just to shock them into slowing down.

After making the run from New Orleans to Natchez in seventeen hours and thirty minutes in 1855, he nailed a large pair of buckhorns on the Natchez dock and painted the time underneath – along with the words, "Take them if you can!" Thomas Paul Leathers was truly a loveable renegade and a hero to the people of Natchez.

In contrast, John Cannon was a quiet, calculating captain. He was born in Kentucky and learned riverboat piloting on the Ouachita River. Cannon had narrowly escaped death when his first steamboat, the *Louisiana,* blew up spectacularly killing 86 people at the port of New Orleans in 1849. It is said that the incident made him all the more vigilant when captaining other ships on the Mississippi.

Cannon was also known as an ambitious businessman who was determined to out-class all competition with his fleet of elegant steamboats on the lower Mississippi. He was a serious entrepreneur and captain, not to be underestimated.

The two steamboats were often compared as to which made a particular run faster, or had the more lavish accommodations, and it wasn't long before an unofficial rivalry sprang up between the two. This was quickly picked up by the local newspapers along the Mississippi, which fueled the fire.

Exactly when and where the die was cast has been lost to

history – both captains had made boastful statements about their respective steamboats, and probably due in a large part to the press, a race was on. It was to be a head-to-head running from New Orleans to St. Louis to settle on one champion between the two boats.

Captain Thomas P. Leathers   Captain John Cannon

Word about the competition spread like wildfire across the nation, even spilling over into Europe. Bookmakers around the world went into overdrive, odds changed by the minute as rumors and stories about the two captains and their steamboats flourished.

The *Robert E. Lee* was docked in New Orleans before the race and while waiting for the *Natchez* to arrive, Captain Cannon took advantage of the extra time. He had the ship stripped of every extra item of weight. Chandeliers, doors, pens for hauling cattle, safety banisters, chains, anchors, furniture, bars and their stock, literally any item that wasn't nailed down or needed for the journey... all of the ship's trappings were

160

removed for the race.

Captain Leathers of the *Natchez* heard about that tactic and not only boasted that he wouldn't stoop to the level of stripping his precious ship, but went on to say that he would take on all passengers and freight and still beat the rival *Robert E. Lee.*

On the morning of the race, June 30, 1870, the port of New Orleans was filled with an audience for the event. Even as the sun rose over Louisiana, Canal Street was packed to the point that it was impassable to even pedestrian traffic. Observers lined every building top and balcony, even though the race was not scheduled to start until 5 PM.

At exactly five in the afternoon, a cannon shot boomed across the river to signal the start of the event. Captain Cannon pulled his ship away from the dock, immediately starting its journey upriver. He felt that any lead on the *Natchez* would be an advantage. His rival, Captain Leathers, pulled out a full five minutes later in pursuit… the race was on. Telegraph operators cabled the information down the line, and the start of the race was noted around the world.

At the first observation point, twenty-five miles upriver from New Orleans, shouts rang out among the people there. The *Robert E. Lee* was leading the race by a full four minutes and forty seconds. The crowd cheered, but what they didn't realize was that the *Natchez* was slowly but surely gaining on her rival.

Both captains looked through their binoculars, searching for the other vessel. Cannon looked for the *Natchez* in his wake, and Leathers watched carefully for the *Lee* up ahead.

Harnett T. Kane described the scene in her book, *Natchez on the Mississippi* in 1947: *"Below decks Tom Leathers stalked around, raging. What was the matter with them all? More of that fat pin, faster! The firemen, naked to the waist, their bodies almost scorched in the heat, wiped the sweat away and jumped into action. Bells rang, the engines beat relentlessly. The wash of the paddles rose in their ears, as the big vessel*

161

seemed to pant with the exertion. Outside, sparks were falling into the water with a hiss. Paint cracked on the deck and now and then flames licked out of the red-hot stacks. Still, Tom Leathers fretted. A whiskey bucket was slapped down, with a tin cup, for everybody knew that made a crew work faster. A barrel of resin was tossed in, and a new roar shook the boat."

The *Natchez* edged up on the *Lee* with every mile that passed. First it was three quarters of an hour, then a half hour, then twenty minutes ahead.

The race continued. In the city of Natchez, the citizens packed the edges of the bluffs the next morning. There was an excitement in the air as rumors and speculation spread throughout the crowd. Finally, just before ten AM, someone spied the smoke from a riverboat coming around the bend. Harnett T. Kane captured the moment in her assessment of the race approaching Natchez, quoting a young boy of the time: "It was a bad time for us. We were running behind. I stood on the shore, watching with the rest, and some people looked like they were crying. But it was such a grand sight, the two boats so close together, and straining with every inch, that we couldn't stay downcast. As the enemy boat came up, we had to shout."

Captain Cannon was leading by under twenty minutes, but he was eyeing another prize. He ordered the *Robert E. Lee* to turn toward the wharf in Natchez, where Captain Leathers' buck antlers were posted for his run of 17 hours and 30 minutes. Since Cannon had beat the time and had made the New Orleans to Natchez run in 17 hours and 11 minutes, he dispatched one of the ship's officers down the dock to snatch the horns and bring them to him. The *Robert E. Lee* then steamed out of Natchez, and the race was getting tight.

Northward on the river there was a stronger current, and many people watching on the race felt that the stripped-down *Lee* would have the advantage. As it turned out, it did. Both ships plowed toward Vicksburg, and Captain Cannon brought his ship there sixteen minutes ahead of the *Natchez*. But then

Cannon brought in one of his most controversial – and brilliant – points of the race. He had the steamer *Frank Pargaud* waiting downriver from Natchez, and it was loaded with the supplies needed for the race, including pine resin and lard.

A postcard commemorating the great race

As the *Robert E. Lee* cleared the city of Natchez, the steamer *Parguad* pulled alongside to unload its supplies. Being lashed to the *Lee* during the process, it kept the steamboat from falling behind during the refueling process.

The two ships continued to battle as they headed upriver, first passing the city of Memphis around midnight, where enormous fires had been ignited along the banks to illuminate the race, then on toward the city of Cairo, Illinois.

Captain Cannon came close to disaster at that particular port. Since the *Natchez* was a full hour behind the *Robert E. Lee* at that point he put into port to unload some of the passengers that were on board.

A pre-victory celebration broke out while they were docked, complete with impromptu dancing and champagne.

163

After a few minutes of revelry, Cannon ordered his ship back out into the river.

Then the unthinkable happened... the ship was stuck on a sandbar. The captain used every bit of experience to maneuver the ship back and forth, slowly rocking it off of its perch and back into open water once again. By the time that he was able to accomplish that feat, the *Natchez* was steaming away in the distance – Captain Leathers had closed the gap.

The two steamships battled it out as they each pressed toward St. Louis, but another twist of fate was lying ahead on the river... a blanket of heavy fog. The ships cut into the soupy haze, both captains fretting over the safety of their steamboats. Unable to see either bank, the twists and turns of the river and sandbars popping up unexpectedly posed a dangerous threat. The entire race could be lost in a wreck – not to mention the lives of the captains and crew.

Captain Leathers decided that discretion was the better part of valor and he ordered that the *Natchez* pull to shore and be tied off until the fog passed. Captain Cannon, on the other hand, pressed ahead; he relied on his memory of the bends of the river, but more importantly, on his good fortune. After a gut-wrenching hour of suspense, slowly making its way through the fog, the *Robert E. Lee* broke into clear air and set full steam for St. Louis.

On July 4th, 1870, at 11:25 AM the *Robert E. Lee* steamed into the destination city to fireworks and a wild celebration. Over six hours later, the *Natchez* pulled into the port of St. Louis, and was given a similar welcome.

Of course, that's where the controversy started. Captain Leathers pointed out that if you subtracted the time that he was tied up to wait out the fog, he had clearly won the race.

Arguments over bets on the race went back and forth, but the New York Times probably best summed up the race on July 6, 1870: "Captain Leathers of the steamer *Natchez* claims that deducting six hours laid up by fog between here and Cairo, and thirty-six minutes lost repairing a pump below Helena, the *Natchez* beat the *Lee's* time some twenty minutes. A banquet to both Captains will be given at the Southern Hotel tonight."

Who knows for sure... only one thing is certain: if you walk into any saloon in Natchez and bring up the subject of the race, you're likely to start a rather loud – and heated – argument about the outcome. The people of Natchez still think highly of the steamship that bore the city's name.

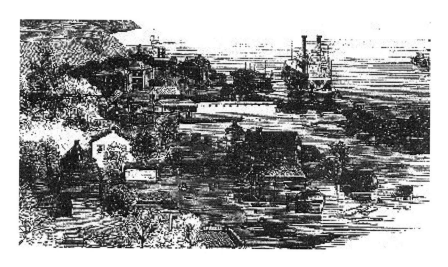

Natchez Under-the-Hill

If you take Silver Street down to the area of town known as "Natchez Under-the-Hill," you'll find an entertaining saloon, a delicious restaurant, perhaps a store or two in which to browse, and a floating casino steamboat with all the amenities. It's a must-see destination for visitors to the city. Back in the 1800s, though, most proper folks wouldn't have dared to venture down below the bluffs. It was known up and down the river as being the most notorious landing on the entire stretch of the Mississippi.

The land under the hill stretched out a few hundred yards to meet the river. It was an irregular shelf of earth that was about three quarters of a mile long, but looked much larger.

The streets ran at odd angles with no rhyme or reason. Shacks and shanties dotted any vacant foot of space; some were used as warehouses, others for much more lucrative pursuits such as gambling, drinking, or other ways of entertaining gentlemen from the boats that docked in Natchez.

One dreadful legend that can't be substantiated is that several of the saloons under the hill were built on piers, and included trap doors with the river flowing underneath. When an unsuspecting stranger came into one of these saloons flashing a roll of money, the bartender would ply him with cheap liquor to entice him to stay until closing. As the bartender issued last call and the patrons were emptying out, the stranger would be clubbed until he was unconscious, his money and other possessions taken, and finally, his body would be fed out through the trap door to splash down into the river. The more fortunate of these would awaken in the light of day miles downstream, but many reportedly slipped to the river bottom to become dinner for the predators there. Whether the legends of the trap door saloons are true or not, Natchez Under-the-Hill was an unsavory place.

In 1874 a book entitled *The Autobiography of Elder Matthew Gardner: A Minister in the Christian Church for Sixty-Three Years* stated, "There were 'under the hill' about forty houses, occupied principally by gamblers and lewd women. These houses were located on a narrow strip of bottom land and there was no place spoken of as a greater sink of sin than 'Natchez Under-the-Hill.'"

Some seventy-something years later in 1947, Harnett T. Kane reflected on those old times in the book *Natchez on the Mississippi*: "The reputation of Under-the-Hill was, in part, less than desirable. Arriving with the cotton, mail, coal and molasses were drunks, bandits, murderers, and other rabble-rousers who, each evening, frequented the brothels, bars, and taverns that dotted Silver Street. Fist and knife fights were considered the norm, and muggings, shootings, and murders were a regular occurrence. One or more murders per evening were not unusual."

In spite of its shady reputation, Natchez Under-the-Hill grew into a thriving port. Along with the illicit trade, legitimate businesses and warehouses began to open. When the sun set over the town of Vidalia, Louisiana, across the river, honest folks had padlocked their shops and gone home, but the fact is, these legitimate places did exist, steadily growing in number.

This caused a new type of business to spring up; mule-carts and their drivers traveled up and down the road from Under-the-Hill to the top of the bluffs and back again, transporting both passengers and freight.

The Bluff City Railway was established to take advantage of this obvious need, and a train went back and forth throughout the day. Ferries also operated between Natchez Under-the-Hill and Vidalia. One ferryboat operator was Jacob Lowe, mentioned in this book's chapter on Rosalie Mansion.

Natchez Under-the-Hill enjoyed prosperity for many years, even though it was like two sides of a coin; there was the ever-present undercurrent of evil, while it continued to grow as a legitimate riverport. Finally, though, the river traffic slowed down. The railroad began to slowly erode the steamship's hold on shipping and transportation, and the impact was felt greatly Under the Hill. The deathblow came in the 1930s, when the U.S. Army Corps of Engineers eliminated an upstream loop on the Mississippi River causing the current to flow faster than it ever had. The outcroppings of Natchez Under-the-Hill were soon consumed by the river, leaving the one main avenue of Silver Street as you see it today.

The Old Natchez Jail

About a block up from the Hanging Tree at 314 State Street is the Old Natchez Jail. It was built in 1891 and became the official location for incarceration... and for executions.

The standard cells were a claustrophobic nightmare – tight quarters with two metal cots, a sink and a toilet. The sink was even squeezed beneath one of the beds. The cramped accommodations were a far cry from some of the plush penitentiaries that exist today. Two side walls were solid iron and the other two consisted of iron bars with heavy crosspieces.

The cells opened up into a central corridor, which was also bounded by heavy bars on each end. Should a criminal escape his cell he would only find himself further trapped in the small hallway. Escape was an unlikely alternative to the lonely days and nights.

169

A typical cell in the Old Natchez Jail

Along with the regular cells for common criminals there was a "death row" built on the second floor. Four tiny cells for those sentenced to death looked directly into the area across the room reserved for the man awaiting execution. All four cells could see the trap door where the condemned man would swing. Part of their punishment was obviously to watch the execution of others, giving them time to contemplate their own demise – it must have been terrible.

As for the man awaiting death, his fate must have played out very slowly. He would be taken to the tiny, solitary cell and locked inside. The other prisoners on "death row" would watch him with hollow, empathetic stares. The trap door with its lethal lever was right in front of him, ever-present in his line of sight.

As the officials began preparing for the execution, he would see the noose tied through a ring in the ceiling, then

170

watch as the lever and metal trap door were tested several times, the clang-thump-clang echoing through the entire building.

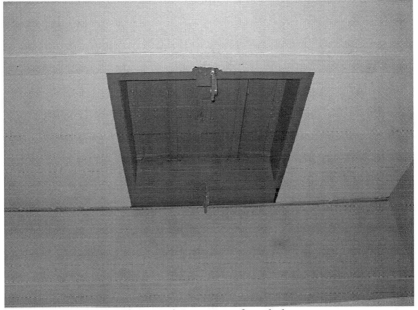

The trap door as seen from below

When they came for him, the condemned was pulled over to stand on the trap door, the noose put around his neck. The verdict was read aloud by an official from the court and after a nod from the sheriff, the executioner would pull the lever.

The fall was a full story, so the problems experienced at the hanging tree didn't happen at the jail – the condemned's neck would break and after a few final spasms, he was dead.

The bottom floor had a large door beneath the trap door for the coroner to bring his wagon. He would be waiting there below, and after a suitable amount of time he would pronounce the death and cut the body down. The corpse would fall into the bed of the wagon, and the coroner would be on his way.

171

This process was repeated time and time again, from the first hanging in 1891 until the last one in 1935.

"Death Row" in the old Natchez Jail

One interesting story about the hangings concerns the executioner himself – a jazz musician named Clarence "Bud" Scott. He was born a slave in the city of Natchez, where he continued to live even though a musical career that took him from New York to Los Angeles and countless places in between.

People in Natchez still talk about Scott's friendship with Police Chief Mike Ryan. The Chief loved Scott's music, and whenever the musician would see the Chief approaching down the street, he would lead his band in a rousing rendition of "My Wild Irish Rose," which was one of the officer's favorite songs.

To the casual observer, it would seem like Scott was

172

simply serenading his influential friend; those supposedly in the know, however, say that during Prohibition it was simply a way for Scott to signal the area taverns that the law was nearby, and they should hide their whiskey.

In the 1940's the Natchez Times reported, "Bud Scott was a product of the sweat-drenched Dixie river towns, and jazz flowed out of his mouth and fingers, out of every wide pore of him, like honey out of a barrel. He played pure, foot-pattin' Dixieland jazz like it's on tape nowhere. Bud sang on the galleried second story of the Natchez Confectionary on summer nights with a megaphone that his ham-like hand nearly swallowed. The gallery seemed to hang in the night sky and it dripped with the evening dew."

Bud Scott was known around the country as one of the leading jazz musicians of his time, yet he applied for another job in the city of Natchez – that of hangman. Condemned criminals might have heard his music ringing through the nightclubs of Natchez, and were probably familiar with his voice and face. Imagine their surprise when they were placed on the trap door of death there in the jail, only to look over and see the musician clutching the lever that would send them into eternity.

The last hanging recorded at the jail was in 1935, but prisoners were housed there until the building closed in 1970. Trustees were hired to live at the jail and guard the inmates, and they often brought their families to live in an apartment in the building. Few trustees stayed longer than a month or two – they complained about the noises that emanated from the cells, especially death row, even when no one was there.

The old jail building is now the Adams County Administration and Board of Supervisors building and has been completely restored. Much of it has been modernized and turned into offices and meeting rooms, but the old death row is still intact.

But the old jail is by no means quiet. Cries, moans, and

labored breathing have been heard within the walls. The apparition of a man in a red shirt has been seen walking the first floor, and no one is exactly sure what might be going on upstairs in death row.

You can walk by the old jail today and imagine some of the macabre events that have taken place there. As you face the right side of the building, look to the jail bars on the right side and gaze into the windows – who knows what you might see.

Natchez City Cemetery

When people tell me that they're going to visit the Natchez City Cemetery, I've stopped asking how long they're going to be there. After all, it doesn't matter a bit – however long you're planning on spending at the cemetery, take my word for it, the time won't be nearly enough. I'm convinced that you could spend a full week out there, wandering through the graves, reading the headstones, and having a very interesting time.

The cemetery was founded in 1822 and today contains thousands of graves (marked and unmarked) in an area that spans almost 100 acres. As you wander through you will see the tombstones from veterans of every American war, giants and socialites from Natchez' past, beside common men and women who have helped to shape history of the city. And as you learn the history of the city, you will find the memorials of the vast majority of the participants buried here.

You can visit a dozen times and on each occasion come away with new stories and experiences from the years of history there. Graves from older cemeteries around Natchez were consolidated here, so you will find plots dating back to 1700s among the rows of headstones.

While you will find your visit to be fascinating, please be aware that this is hallowed ground. Take away nothing but photos and bring nothing more than your interest. Several years ago the cemetery put out a list of visitors' guidelines:

The Natchez City Cemetery is one of the most beautiful cemeteries in the South. Please help us maintain its beauty by observing the following rules:

1. Please stay in the designated walkways and do not disturb memorials or artifacts.

2. Please show respect for the dead and for their families. Do not intrude on funeral or memorial services. Do not bring alcohol, fireworks, firearms or entertainment items (radios, CD Players, etc.) into the cemetery.

3. Go-carts and ATV's are not permitted.

4. Well-behaved children under the direct supervision of responsible adults are always welcome. Please teach your children to respect cemeteries.

5. Keep your pets under control on a leash and please clean-up after them.

6. Please do not disturb the wildlife that inhabits the cemetery.

7. Please do not litter. (This includes cigarette butts, chewing gum, etc.) Trash receptacles are located throughout the cemetery for your convenience.

8. Artificial flowers will be removed as soon as they are faded. All flowers shall be secured in an urn or unbreakable vase attached to or placed on the monument.

9. Pinwheels, wind chimes, glass vases and jars, solar devices and other decorative objects are not permitted. One statue per plot is permitted. Exceptions will be made for the American Flag.

10. Please register group activities in advance with the director.

11. No additions and/or improvements to lots (i.e. bench's, Landscaping, Walls, etc) shall be made without express approval of the beautification committee of the Natchez City Cemetery Association
12. No spreading of Cremation Ashes.
Please treat these sacred graves and grounds with respectful reverence they deserve. Thank you for leaving our Historic Cemetery not worse, but better for your presence.

With one visit to the cemetery, you will quickly become one of its advocates. It is hard not to fall in love with the beauty and history of this hallowed ground.

Dotting the cemetery are hexagon pavilions such as the one in the first photo of this chapter. At one time, there were gutters on the roofs that channeled rainwater into cisterns in the center of each structure that made drinking water available to cemetery visitors of the past. The benches under the roof also gave people a place to rest during funerals or simple visits.

One of the best ways to experience the cemetery is simply to park your car and start walking and reading, here are some of the most interesting places in the cemetery to visit:

The Loving Caretaker
Just after entering the front gate, on your right you'll see a cross-shaped gravestone belonging to Frances Fitzallen Reily, born on September 12, 1878, and who died on July 3, 1937. The inscription on the stone reads, *My Sweetheart – My Pal – My Wife*; it was erected by her husband Louis Hartman Lawrence.

After his wife's death, he is said to have visited her grave every day with his toolbox. He would first say a prayer, then step inside the concrete boundary where he would clean the tombstone, clip the grass, and make sure that his beloved wife's grave was perfectly cared for. Sometimes he left the toolbox there, and more than once, cemetery workers found

177

him sleeping on the ground beside his wife's grave.

They eventually put up a bench where he could rest and under which he could leave his toolbox. Louis continued this ritual until his death in 1960 at the age of eighty-four years. Just imagine that – for twenty-three years he visited his wife and cared for her grave.

He now rests beside his bride, and if you visit the grave, you will find that it is still well-manicured and his toolbox rests beneath the bench for all time, a fitting memorial to the love between a husband and a wife.

The Civil War Casualty

Rosalie Beekman was the only Civil War casualty in Natchez that resulted directly from a Union attack. Seven-year-old Rosalie and her family were fleeing up Silver Street when the federal gunboat U.S.S. Essex shelled Natchez on September 2nd, 1862. Her parents, Aaron and Fanny Beekman operated a business Under-the-Hill, and fled the cannonfire to the safety of the top of the bluffs. One story reports that she fell upon being struck by a piece of shrapnel, and her father called back for her to get up. According to that account, she called out, "I can't, Papa, I'm killed!" He ran back and scooped her into his arms to take her to safety, but young Rosalie died the next day.

The inscription on her headstone reads:

The summons came forth and she died.
Yet her parting was gentle, for those
Whom she loved mingled tears at her side.
Her death was dear Rosa's repose;
Out weakness may weep o'er her bier,
But her spirit has gone on the wing
To triumph for agony here,
To rejoice in the joy of her king.

The Name Says It All...

According to local legend, Louise was a prostitute who worked in a brothel down under the hill after the Civil War. There are many colorful stories about the poor girl; some say that she came to town, a talented lady of the evening who made a good living down at the docks. Others argue that her fiancée had abandoned her in town without any means to get by, and prostitution became her only way to survive. Whatever the case, most people believe that she was one of the city's "tainted angels" who spent her entire life at Natchez Under-the-Hill.

In any case, she reportedly died of tuberculosis and was buried in the city cemetery. One story says that she became friends with the doctor who was treating her during her illness, and that he paid for her grave and funeral. Yet another espouses that one of her wealthy clients took care of the burial expenses because he had fallen in love with her. No matter what the case, the poor lady was buried with the simple tombstone epitaph, "Louise the Unfortunate," and the actual meaning is anyone's guess. It is one of the mysteries of the Natchez City Cemetery.

The Namesake Of Vidalia

Don José Vidal was born on March 12, 1763 in Coruña, Spain, and came to serve his country in the Spanish holdings in North America, specifically, in the Mississippi Territory. Of the many titles that he held, from 1792 to 1797 he was the secretary to Manuel Gayoso de Lemos, the Spanish Governor of the Natchez District.

In 1798 the United States was taking over the Mississippi Territory – including Natchez – from Spain. José Vidal, wanted to continue to live on Spanish territory so he petitioned the Spanish Governor, General Manuel Gayoso de Lemos, for a land grant across the river from the city Natchez. His petition was granted, but with one major stipulation: Vidal was obligated to establish a fort on the property, which he did. Don José moved his entire family from the city Natchez to their new home across the Mississippi River, where he became the Spanish Commandant of the new Post of Concord.

As has happened throughout history, the fort attracted settlers and businessmen, and a city began to grow on that side of the river. It was named Vidalia, after Don José Vidal. He lived there until his death in 1823.

The Doctor and the Slave-Prince

Here rests the honorable Dr. John Coates Cox, who lived from 1762 to 1816. Dr. Cox, an Irish doctor visiting Africa as a ship's surgeon in the 1780s, found himself abandoned when his ship sailed for home without him.

Suffering from disease and near starvation, he was rescued by a local tribe and spent a year as the guest of King Sori and the royal African family who ruled the region. When he left, he was sent to the coast of West Africa with an escort from the royal family; from there he sailed to England, and then settled in America... specifically, the riverport city of Natchez.

Some time before, a plantation owner named Thomas Foster of Natchez had purchased two slaves for about a thousand dollars. In 1807 Dr. Cox happened to see one of these slaves, and recognized him as Ibrahima, the son of King Sori who had been his host many years before. Dr. Cox immediately tried to persuade Foster that his slave was of royal blood, but to no avail. He offered to purchase Ibrahima for a sum as high as one thousand dollars, but the offer fell on deaf ears. Thomas Foster did start to refer to the slave as "Prince," and the legends of his background began to spread. In fact, Ibrahima became one of the country's most well-known slaves.

182

The doctor, feeling an obligation to the royal African family that had saved him, launched a crusade to free Ibrahima that would last several years and involved many prominent people in Natchez.

Foster and Ibrahima saw each other often for nine years until, unfortunately, Dr. John Cox passed away in 1816. His son William continued the quest for the freedom of the Prince-slave on behalf of his father. In 1826, while an international push was on to free the Prince, Thomas Foster set the man and his wife free.

Ibrahima tried to raise the funds to free his children as well, but obtained the money to free only a portion of his family before his ship was set to sail for Africa. Sadly, before he was able to return home, Ibrahima died from a long illness.

The grave of Dr. John Coates Cox, however, remains as a testament to someone who saw beyond the bounds of slavery and worked to free a man of noble descent.

The Chinese Gambler

One of the most unique modern monuments in the cemetery belongs to a merchant from the city of Ferriday, Louisiana named John Lee, Sr. The city is home to other notables such as singer Jerry Lee Lewis and evangelist Jimmy Swaggart. Since John Lee owned and operated the Pick and Pay Restaurant in Ferriday since it was opened in 1925, there is a good chance that he entertained both men in his establishment and possibly even their Cousin, Mickey Gilley, who was born in nearby Natchez.

Lee was a man who enjoyed a good game of chance, and in fact, was known as the "Chinese gambler." Born on August 15th, 1892, he died at the age of seventy years on July 11th, 1962.

He was buried in the Natchez City Cemetery and his headstone is one that is extremely interesting to examine.

The Chinese lettering on either side reads, "Good Fortune." The cards across the top show an ace-high straight flush, also known as a "Royal Flush," which is the highest standard poker hand. It is in the suite of spades, which is considered to be the highest of the four suites.

The dice on the left side of the stone have been rolled to a four-three "seven," and the dice on the right side have been rolled to a five-six "eleven." Of course, if rolled on the "come out" – or first – roll, the player is a winner.

These things alone are good icons for a gambling man, but there is something even more interesting about Mr. Lee's monument – his date of death was in July, the seventh month, on the eleventh day; he literally rolled a seven-eleven on his deathbed.

A Love Story Across The Sea

Count Casimir dem Bouski was born to the nobility of Poland, and spent much of it traveling. He served in the Pontifical Zouaves at the Vatican, the elite fighting force that defended the Holy Father and the Holy See. While in Rome he met a young lady named Gertrude Holmes who was traveling abroad with her father. They began spending time together, first as friends but the couple soon fell deeply in love.

When they announced their betrothal, her father vehemently objected – he didn't want his daughter to fall for a whirlwind romance with a foreigner who had so many cultural differences. Her father took her back to America immediately, but not before they met one last time where the Count pledged to stay faithful to their love.

He threw his attention to military endeavors to take his mind off his Gertrude. He joined a legion of men who were going to attempt to seize the city of Venice. When they failed, the men were exiled and the Count fled to America, landing in New Orleans.

He found work aboard a steamboat under an assumed name, hoping to one day find his love in her native country. Before the ship reached the city of Natchez, the Count fell ill with a fever. He died, but not before telling the Captain his story and asking him to contact Gertrude. Count Casmir dem Bouski died, and his body was taken ashore at Natchez.

The ship's captain contacted the French Curate there, and told him the sad tale of dem Bouski and his love. The Curate had the Count buried at the city cemetery, and then penned a letter to Gertrude in Philadelphia, her home. He explained the circumstances of the Count's death, and told her of his faithful love.

Some time later, a woman dressed in mourning clothes came to visit the Curate. She greeted him with the words, "I am Gertrude." She was taken to her true love's grave, which she later enclosed in an iron fence, and erected a stone that said:

Count Gasmir Dem Bouski
Zouave Pontifical
Died June 30, 1869
Age 25 years
I shall go to him but he shall not return to me. ~ Gertrude

A Potential Case Of Poison

John Anthony Quitman was a lawyer and planter who arrived in Natchez in 1820. He married a proper lady named Eliza Turner and purchased Monmouth where the couple began their lives together.

They had eleven children together, and over the course of his life John held many offices; he served in the Mississippi House of Representatives, was a delegate to the Mississippi state constitutional convention, a member of Mississippi state senate, the Governor of Mississippi, a state court judge, and a

General in the U.S. Army during the Mexican War.

Quitman died at Monmouth in 1858; the official word was that it was dysentery. It is said, however, that he had been deliberately poisoned at a banquet during the inauguration of President James Buchanan, in Washington, D.C.

There may be some truth to that claim, because many who attended became ill. The owner of the hotel where the banquet was held was a supporter, so the President felt safe in holding the state affair there. But by the next morning, President Buchanan was so sick that there was question as to whether he could give the inaugural address. He remained ill for weeks, as did many of the people at the party. Quitman was the only attendee who died.

There were rumors in some extreme pro-South circles that the poisoning was a plot to remove the new Democratic administration, but such talk was quickly hushed.

The blame was put on various things: sewer gas escaping into the room, the hotel pipes freezing in the winter causing a sewage backup into the kitchen contaminating food, or rats in the hotel dying and falling into the water supply.

Whatever the true cause was, John Anthony Quitman, public servant and war hero, died in his home on June 17, 1858, and in the final days required assistance to even move.

The Musician And Hangman

Clarence "Bud" Scott was born a slave in the city of Natchez, a place that he continued to call home even though his musical career took him across the United States. He played with some of the best jazz musicians in the world in places like New York, Los Angeles, Chicago and many other American hotspots.

He took to music early in life, choosing the mandolin as his first instrument. Before long he was playing almost any musical instrument that he picked up. His love for music expanded into composing and arranging pieces. In time he

188

assembled a group of musicians into one of the most popular orchestras to play along the Mississippi River region.

An article in the Natchez Times Newspaper said, on the occasion of Scott's death, "Bud Scott was a product of the sweat-drenched Dixie river towns, and jazz flowed out of his mouth and fingers, out of every wide pore of him, like honey out of a barrel. He played pure, foot-tappin' Dixieland jazz like it's on tape nowhere.

The odd thing about Bud Scott was that he applied for the job of hangman in the city of Natchez, a position that he won. Many of the men that he sent into eternity were probably ones that had been dancing to his music months before. When Bud Scott passed away in 1938, the jazz world grieved and he was buried in Natchez City Cemetery. His headstone has only his name and birth/death years on one side, and on the other, a simple musical note.

Afraid Of Thunderstorms

The sad tale behind this next grave begins when a little girl named Florence Irene Ford died of yellow fever at the tender age of ten.

Her family was devastated – especially her mother. Mrs.

Ford could not bear the thought of placing her daughter alone below the cold dirt of the cemetery. Since that couldn't be prevented, she did the next best thing. At her instruction, a custom coffin was built for little Florence that had a glass window to display her body.

The grave was also out of the ordinary – at one end, a set of concrete steps leading down beneath the ground was installed with heavy iron doors to cover them. At the bottom, a glass wall was put in so that Mrs. Ford could see her daughter's windowed coffin.

The mother could descend the stairs any time that she wished to see her daughter. Because Florence Irene was so frightened of thunderstorms, Mrs. Ford would go out to the cemetery any time that it rained, walking down the steps, sitting there with her daughter's body.

Mrs. Ford finally passed away herself, and the glass wall

to the grave was sealed with concrete to prevent vandalism. The steps are still there, and when you visit the cemetery, you can walk down them yourself. At the bottom, you'll be facing the concrete wall – little Florence is just a few inches on the other side.

There apparently are some ghost stories associated with the cemetery as well – take this one concerning Florence Irene Ford's grave, reported by the Natchez Democrat, and reproduced here with their kind permission:

Young Girl's Grave Is Haunted, Some Locals, Visitors Say

By Julie Finley
The Natchez Democrat
Oct 30, 2006
(used here with permission of The Natchez Democrat)

The facts alone are creepy.

A young girl dies before her time. Her mother is unable to let go and has a walk-in grave built.

The woman spends each night sitting underground, facing the glass wall that separates her from her daughter. She sings, reads, anything to comfort a child who was afraid of the dark.

Iron flaps up top can close or open to protect mother and daughter from winds and rain.

And the stuffed animals are buried on the other side of the glass too.

But it's not the facts that give longtime cemetery director Don Estes the heebie-jeebies.

Estes, now retired from the director job, doesn't believe in ghosts. He's walked the roads at the Natchez City Cemetery at night many a time. And he's never seen a flying orb.

But the 1871 grave of Florence Irene Ford makes him believe – sort of.

Five cement steps lead down to the glass window – which

191

has since been bricked over.

Estes routinely gives tours of the cemetery and the grave of 10-year-old Ford.

"I brought a lady out here one time, and she just got frantic," he said.

"Twelve years ago her mother had brought her here. Her mother went down the steps and came out screaming, rolling on the ground with a green glow all over her."

The young woman told Estes how a cemetery worker at the time witnessed the glow. After a few minutes it began to fade. The worker bent down and scooped it off, making a ball he could hold in his hands.

He later released it into the air, where it went up, sparkled and disappeared, Estes said.

Sensible Estes didn't quite believe and began some research of his own.

He found the cemetery worker, Mr. Davis.

"He told me the exact same story," Estes said. "He said it felt like compressed air or like a tennis ball in his hand."

The account was so similar, that Estes became a believer, he said.

"I believe because I had an actual testimony of an actual man, and I had it verified and I didn't prompt him in any way," Estes said.

But Jacqueline Stephens, who runs Ghost Tours with her husband, has even more evidence, she says.

Stephens uses a cell sensor to detect electromagnetic waves, energy and, well, ghosts.

She didn't get any positive readings Monday night – 135 years after Irene died, to the day – but she has before.

"I got three readings one time, right in the center," she said. "The best reading came down the steps."

A positive cell sensor reading falls at about the number 5 on the sensor's scale. The detector can be affected by electricity and streetlights, but Estes says there are no outlets

near Irene's grave.
And that's not good for Irene. The little girl was, after all, afraid of the dark.

The Steps Leading Down To Florence Irene Ford's Grave

Buried Sitting Up

One rather large – and unusual – monument that is located off of Steamboat Street in the cemetery is inscribed with the following epitaph:

Sacred to the memory of Rufus E. Case,
who died at Wallenstein, La, November 29th, 1858.
Aged 31 Years & 8 Months.
Thy Will Not Mine, O Lord.

By our standards, Rufus was quite a young man, dying at the early age of thirty-one. While we don't know much about him or how he died, his memorial is one of the more unique ones in the cemetery.

The monument is in three tiers – three boxes really, that look as if they were stacked on top of each other. According to the book *Historic Natchez City Cemetery*, the reason behind this is that Rufus wanted to be buried in his favorite rocking chair, facing his Louisiana home. A child in his family had died before him and so his rocking chair was positioned beside the young one's grave and the tomb was built around him. Rufus is forever looking out toward the Mississippi River.

If you sit on the first tier of the monument, facing the Mississippi River, keep in mind that except for a few inches of concrete, you will basically be sitting in the dead man's lap.

Visitors to the cemetery do this all the time and all describe a definite chill while sitting there. Perhaps it is Rufus, just letting you know that he's still there.

The Steamship Captain

Captain Thomas P. Leathers was a native of the state of Kentucky, who owned and operated eight different steamships named "Natchez." The good captain began his river career on the Yazoo River in 1836, and became quite an accomplished steamship pilot. He drove the Natchez VI for 401 trips without accident in the New Orleans to Vicksburg trade route – a great accomplishment, especially during a time where there was little or no safety regulations for river-going vessels.

In 1870 as owner and captain of the Natchez, Thomas P. Leathers participated in what was to become the most legendary steamboat race in the history of the mighty Mississippi, running his ship against the notorious Captain Cannon and his Robert E. Lee. The race is described in detail in another chapter of this book.

195

Even though he officially lost the race, Captain Leathers was a man who was well-respected in the city of Natchez. His money was no good in any of the town's taverns; gentlemen clamored to buy him drinks, eager to hear the details of the great race over and over.

Tragically, Captain Thomas P. Leathers died in the city of New Orleans at the age of 80. He was involved in an accident where he was run over by a bicyclist. That terrible incident ended one of the most successful careers in the history of steamboats on the Mississippi.

The Yellow Duchess

In this family plot, one grave is covered by an enormous concrete tomb that dominates everything else around it – that is the resting place of Natchez' famous "Yellow Duchess," Katherine Lintot Minor.

She was married to Major Stephen Minor, the last Spanish Governor in Natchez, and they lived at Concord Mansion. Major Minor (sorry I couldn't resist that) had purchased the house and estate in 1800 for the sum of $10,000.

Katherine earned her nickname as the Yellow Duchess because of her fondness for the color yellow. From her blond hair to her bright yellow carriage, she tried to work the hue into all aspects of her life. The gardens at Concord were filled with yellow roses and the furniture and décor in the home were yellow as well. This extended to her wardrobe and her jewelry was, of course, gold. It has even been said that the horses pulling her carriage were Golden Palominos and that her personal slaves were mulatto.

The huge monument over her grave was reportedly put there to prevent grave robbery – apparently Katherine was buried with quite a bit of her jewelry.

The Yellow Duchess' epitaph reads:

> *Sacred to the memory of Katherine Lintot,*
> *Daughter of Bernard & Katherine Lintot,*

and relict of the late Major Stephen Minor.
Born in Connecticut on the fourth of Aug, 1770.
She died at her residence (Concord) in
Adams County Mississippi,
on the ninth of July 1844.
Aged 74 years.
In all the relations of life she was as near perfect
as mortals are permitted to become.

The Turning Angel

There is a statue of an angel at the front of the cemetery that, as you approach from a particular angle, appears to turn to greet you. It has been the subject of Natchez legend throughout the years... but the thing about it is, this legend is true. Because of this, the statue has been dubbed, "The Turning Angel."

In this case, there is a logical explanation. If you read the inscription on the stature, it says: *Erected by the Natchez Drug*

197

Company to the memory of the unfortunate employees who lost their lives in the great disaster that destroyed its building on march 14, 1908.

The five girls who were killed are buried under the watchful gaze of the angel.

The Natchez Drug Company commissioned the statue, and the artist carved it in such a way to form an optical illusion. Approaching the statue from the correct angle makes it appear to turn as you grow nearer. What is that angle? To be honest, I don't know, and I've never been able to figure it out.

I've come at her from every conceivable path, and I've still never seen the angel turn. It is still a beautiful monument, one of the most famous in the cemetery.

Bestselling author Greg Iles even wrote a book about a murder in Natchez with the title, *Turning Angel*. It is truly an icon of the city, and a beautiful memorial to the five girls whose lives were tragically lost in the fire.

Make plans to visit Natchez City Cemetery – it is a place of peace and rest that solemnly reflects the history of the old city. Each marker represents a human life and has its own unique story.

There are many powerful things to consider while walking down the rows of gravestones in the cemetery. This chapter only gives a few of the tales there, hopefully serving as a springboard for your visit. My wish is that you will visit the cemetery, stroll quietly among the markers there, contemplating not only the history of Natchez, but the lives of those individuals who helped to build this beautiful city.

Remember, though, that the cemetery is hallowed ground. Enjoy it, but please respect it. Take nothing away but photographs and memories. When you go to visit, you might even bring a few flowers with you. When a particular gravestone moves you, leave one for its owner. They'll be looking down from above and you might just make them smile.

The map on the next page will direct you to the markers discussed in this chapter.

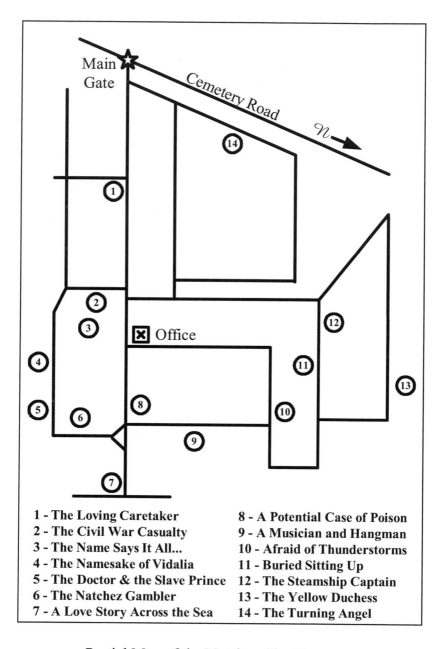

1 - The Loving Caretaker
2 - The Civil War Casualty
3 - The Name Says It All...
4 - The Namesake of Vidalia
5 - The Doctor & the Slave Prince
6 - The Natchez Gambler
7 - A Love Story Across the Sea

8 - A Potential Case of Poison
9 - A Musician and Hangman
10 - Afraid of Thunderstorms
11 - Buried Sitting Up
12 - The Steamship Captain
13 - The Yellow Duchess
14 - The Turning Angel

Partial Map of the Natchez City Cemetery

The Natchez Eola Hotel

It's hard to visit Natchez without noticing the Eola Hotel. It is the largest building downtown, standing at seven stories tall, only two blocks from the Mississippi River. It is a historic part of the city's past, opening its doors on July 1, 1927. The newspapers of the day hailed the grand opening as a "symbol of civic progress." The hotel was named after the daughter of Isidore Levy, the president of the board of directors of the Natchez Investment Corporation, the organization that envisioned and built the hotel. The daughter of Isidore was Eola, and her name was destined to become inscribed in the history of the town forever.

The stock market crash of 1929 became the first road bump in the story of the hotel – the Natchez Investment Corporation defaulted on the mortgage payments, and it was put on the market. Interested parties formed a corporation to take over the hotel, and it soon became the property of the Natchez Eola Corporation, with Clarence Eyrich, Sr. as its head. It was the first time, but not the last, that the property would be saved from financial ruin.

In 1932, the Eola became the headquarters for the Natchez Spring Pilgrimage. The Eyrich family, along with other supporters of the grand old hotel, brought in flowers to lavishly decorate the public areas of the hotel during the Historic Pilgrimage; it was booked for many months in advance. During that time it catered to the locals as well as visitors; its coffee shop served twenty-four hours a day. It became a regular meeting place for the citizens of Natchez.

Soon the Eola became "the place" in Natchez for everyone in town to be seen — national celebrities such as Elizabeth Taylor, Montgomery Clift, Tom Mix, Eleanor Roosevelt, and General Douglas MacArthur were counted among its guests.

202

Anyone who was anyone, if they were visiting Natchez, stayed at the Eola Hotel.

It prospered for decades, until business slowed during the 1960s. The Eola closed its doors on November 30, 1974, but like the legendary phoenix arising from the ashes, the hotel was reborn in 1978 under new ownership by the Eola Hotel Corporation. A wave of restoration ensued at a cost of well over six million dollars, but it returned the hotel to the grandeur of its heyday.

The lobby remains where it has always been, with its marble trim, archways, columns, and chandeliers still present. The old coffee shop has been replaced with Café LaSalle, the Eola's formal dining room. A new garden restaurant, Juleps, looks out into the courtyard with its fountain and gaslights. Peacocks Bar & Grill is very popular with the locals of Natchez, and is the perfect spot to unwind with your favorite beverage.

The restoration efforts remained so true to the original construction of the hotel that it was awarded a listing on the National Register of Historic Places. It has also been selected as a Historic Hotel of America by the National Trust for Historic Preservation – the only hotel with that designation in Mississippi, and one of only sixty hotels in America so named.

The story of the hotel hasn't always been a pleasant one. A tragedy hit in 1998, when a tornado ripped through Natchez, struck the hotel and caused over thirty million dollars worth of damage. In fact, it removed the roof and top floor of the Eola. With expert restoration, however, the hotel was returned to its original beauty.

If you visit the Eola today you will see exquisite chandeliers, ornate columns, arched doorways and elaborate appointments much as it might have looked in the bygone days of Natchez. Some rooms have a view of the Mississippi River, while others look over the city. A New Orleans courtyard off of the lobby is a fine appointment to the hotel, featuring a fire and water fountain that will intrigue any guest.

The ultimate in luxury is exemplified by the Moonflower Suites located on the top floor. They are considered to be some of Natchez' most elegant accommodations featuring a beautiful, panoramic view of the Mississippi River.

The Natchez Eola Hotel
110 Pearl Street
Natchez, MS 39120
601.445.6000
www.natchezeola.com

"I'm Afraid Something Terrible Has Happened..."

On August 4th, 1932, those words began an episode of Natchez history that would catch the attention of the entire nation. It began with a gristly murder that soon turned into an investigation with a carnival-like atmosphere. I'll be quick to say that this entire book could be filled with the twists and turns of the event, so please allow me to distill it down to its simplest – and most interesting – points.

The story actually started with four friends, all members of Natchez' elite society. Jane Surget Merrill and Duncan Minor were cousins; Richard Dana was the son of a well-to-do Episcopal minister, and Octavia Dockery was the daughter of a wealthy New York businessman.

Jane Surget Merrill was born in Natchez in 1864, and came from a long line of wealth. Her father, Ayres Phillips Merrill, had amassed a fortune on his own. During the Civil War, he protected his riches by siding with the Union to protect his holdings. Even though it angered the townsfolk, Ayres welcomed the northern invaders that occupied Natchez, especially a distant cousin named Ulysses S. Grant.

When Grant became President of the United States, he repaid Ayres Merrill's kindness by appointing him Ambassador to Belgium; the family's wealth continued to grow.

Jane Surget Merrill's education began in New York, and continued in Europe. She grew into a beautiful young woman who was presented to Queen Victoria at the Court of St. James's during her father's tenure in Europe. Ayres Merrill eventually became too ill to fulfill his ambassador appointment, so Jane brought him back to Natchez, where she took her place as a society woman.

As she aged, Jane became a bit of a recluse in her home, Glenburnie. When she did drive into town, she would pull her Model T in front of a store and honk the horn for salespeople to come out and take care of her shopping needs. Visitors to her house were greeted by a sign that read: *No Admittance. Merrill. Inquire Elsewhere for Persons of Other Names.* Apparently only her cousin Duncan Minor was allowed to enter.

Duncan Minor was born in Natchez in 1862, two years before his cousin. They were fast friends as children, but their separation while Jane was in Europe must have kindled a bit more than friendship. Upon her return to Natchez, Duncan and Jane – or Jennie, as she preferred – took up a full-blown romance.

Richard "Dick" Dana was also a Natchez native, born in 1871. He was the son of the Rector of Trinity Episcopal Church, Dr. Charles Backus Dana. He grew up moving in the same circles as Jennie and Duncan, and became friends with them. As a young man Dick was very talented musically; he studied piano, developing into an accomplished musician. Most people who heard him predicted that he would have a career as a concert pianist.

Sadly, a tragic accident would change his life forever. While lowering a window, the sash came down on his right hand, crushing two fingers, ending any hope of a musical career.

After studying at Vanderbilt University, Dick returned to Natchez and took up residence in the family mansion named Glenwood. It was located next door to Glenburnie. The house was lavishly furnished, including many items from Robert E. Lee, an old friend of the family. Dick became friends with a young lady named Octavia Dockery, and their early relationship was flirtatious, although not romantic.

Octavia came from a well-to-do New York family. She was educated at the prestigious Comstock School for Girls, and took her place in society. At the age of sixteen she was escorted to a prestigious ball by President Ulysses S. Grant.

As a young lady, Octavia became a writer, and her work was published in several periodicals. She followed her sister to Mississippi, where she met Dick Dockery. Both were students of the arts; Dick the pianist, and Octavia the writer/poet.

All four people experienced economic downturns in their lives as they grew older. This is the time when Jennie started her downward spiral into being an eccentric recluse. Duncan was her only visitor; every evening he would come to call at Glenburnie, the only guest that she would receive. He would leave sometime in the morning hours. Gossip spread about the pair – many were sure that they were sharing an intimate relationship, and some even whispered that they had been secretly married.

Octavia moved into Glenwood with her friend Dick Dana, and started raising livestock to make money, including chickens, cows and goats. She was quick to point out that there was nothing romantic between them.

Perhaps the biggest slide came from Dick Dana, who appeared to be losing his mind. He seemed perpetually

207

confused, forgetting the names and identities of friends and neighbors. On one occasion, Octavia found that Dick had cut arm and head holes in a potato sack and was wearing it in lieu of standard clothing. He allowed his hair and beard to grow long and unkempt, giving him a strange, frightening look.

People began to refer to him as "the Wild Man," and to Octavia, because of her farm animals, as "the Goat Woman." The two let Glenwood slowly slip into disrepair.

Next door at Glenburnie, Jennie Merrill was starting to have problems with her former friends. Octavia's goats had started wandering into Jennie's flower garden for a snack.

Vicious notes were exchanged between the two ladies over the invasion of the goats. Tensions escalated, until Jennie finally had enough. She reportedly grabbed a rifle one day, and shot several of the goats that were on her property, and the matter was taken to court.

Glenburnie, home of Jennie Merrill

As Octavia and Dick spiraled further into poverty, fortune changed once again for Jennie. She began to slowly build her wealth back up; by 1932, things were going well for her.

On August 4th of that year, Duncan was making his nightly visit to Glenburnie, but on that evening he found a horrific scene. Blood was spattered all over the entryway; in one corner there was a man's overcoat, also covered in blood.

Many think that it was Duncan who made the famous phone call to the police, "I'm afraid something terrible has happened."

A search for Jennie was launched throughout the evening, but it wasn't until the sun began to rise that someone found her barefoot body. She had been shot through the head and the chest.

The police began arresting anyone in sight who was at all suspicious, including the neighbors Octavia and Dick. When the authorities showed up at Glenwood, Dick Dana was found upstairs washing out what appeared to be a blood-stained shirt. Even though there were many suspects most suspicion was cast at Octavia Dockery and Dick Dana.

Because of the high-society names involved in the case, the local media flocked to Glenwood. The case was brought to national attention when reporters were given a tour of the house.

It was literally in shambles; doors and windows were hanging open, dust covered every surface, and animals roamed freely through the rooms and halls. Chickens nested on most any flat surface and the floors were covered with droppings from the animals. The stench might have been overbearing, if it were not for the ventilation provided by the broken windows throughout the house.

The wallpaper had been eaten away by the goats, as had many of the books, including volumes that had once belonged to Robert E. Lee. The press dubbed the house *Goat Castle*, and the name not only stuck, but created a media frenzy.

209

When she was interviewed in the city jail, Octavia addressed the poor living conditions of Glenwood. "I couldn't help it. It was drudgery, morning to night. I had no time. I had to earn our living. Do you know I had to walk nearly three miles just to get our drinking water?" She denied any knowledge of the murder, however.

The case against the pair was soon strengthened when a handprint was found at the scene that indicated the killer had a deformed hand – much like Dick's, that had been crushed by the falling window.

Another wrinkle to the case came when one witness said that he'd seen a man wearing an overcoat walking around the grounds of Glenburnie that evening, but he could not provide an adequate description.

The overcoat was traced to a small shack on Dick Dana's property called *The Skunks' Nest*. They rented it out to bring in extra income, and the coat had reportedly been left by a previous tenant, a white man working as a logger.

As police reconstructed that day for Dick Dana, they found that just before the murder he was playing piano at Auburn there in Natchez. While they calculated that he could have made it from there to the Skunks' Nest to get the overcoat, and then to Glenburnie to commit the crime; he would have had to do so at a dead run, something that would not have gone unnoticed.

Two additional sets of fingerprints were found at the crime scene, and the case against Octavia and Dick began to slowly unravel. The authorities were hesitant to give up their suspects even though there was a swelling of local support for the pair.

The spotlight turned back onto Duncan Minor when Jennie's will was discovered in a stack of papers at Glenburnie. When the police demanded to see the document, Duncan refused. He was threatened with legal prosecution, though, and finally acquiesced. The will left everything, including Glenburnie, to Duncan, with Jennie's notation, "He knows my wishes and will carry them out accordingly."

Speculation was going wild. Some felt that Duncan was involved, others still looked to Octavia and Dick, while the rest chased wild theories about strangers passing through town or people with grudges against Jennie or her family.

The case was finally blown wide open when a criminal named George Pearls was shot by police in Pine Bluff, Arkansas; his weapon was a .32 caliber pistol and he had a deformed right hand. Papers found on his body indicated that he had been in Natchez recently, and since the Pine Bluff law enforcement had heard that a similar weapon had been used in the unsolved Natchez murder, an offer to share information was made. A test by crime scene experts showed that the weapon had also been used to kill Jane (Jennie) Surget Merrill.

The papers on Pearls' body led Natchez investigators to a woman named Emily Burns, owner of a local boarding house where he had stayed. After an intense interrogation by police, Burns admitted accompanying Pearls to Glenburnie where he hoped that Jennie would make him a loan. She refused, and a confrontation ensued. Pearls, who had been wearing the overcoat taken from the Skunks' Nest, pulled his .32, shot Jennie dead, then hid her body in the nearby brush.

Octavia and Dick were free, but still in the public eye. They decided to make the best of the situation, and started giving tours of "Goat Castle" to Natchez tourists. On occasion, Dick would treat visitors to an impromptu piano recital, and Octavia would regale them with readings of her poetry.

Dick Dana and Octavia Dockery battled poverty and eviction for years, continuing to bring in some money from those curious about the trial and the notorious Goat Castle.

Dick died in 1948 from pneumonia, followed by his companion Octavia about a year later. The regal mansion once known as Glenwood, now nationally called Goat Castle, was in such bad shape that it was torn down after an auction to sell anything salvageable to souvenir-seekers.

An account of a visit to Goat Castle is given in the book, *Natchez on the Mississippi*:

**From *Natchez on the Mississippi*
By Harnett T. Kane**
William Morrow & Co., New York, 1947

"A few months ago, I revisited Goat Castle. The approach is over the wildest terrain in the countryside. Crossing a rickety bridge, my car found a place between one from California, another from Connecticut. Dick Dana, hair awry, beard mussed, bowed with a flourish and his voice tumbled out in a flood of sentences, none bearing much relation to another: 'This fine religious painting – the basis for challenging comparative religion.' He pointed to a broken chair: 'This condition is due to a storm. Now take the Commodore Perry expedition. Do you know my father went to Virginia in 1836? This house, now, it's in a sympathetic situation. This is a historic bed, used by General Lee. Note the steel engraving, representing the marriage of Pocahontas. Some day I intend to catalogue my periodicals.' (These pile six feet high; Dick seldom throws a paper or magazine away.) 'Somehow, in my busy life, I have never had the time.'"

"He seemed in a race with himself; his voice grew strident, as if he were afraid he was not receiving full attention. He got little enough; the tourists, unable to follow the farrago of words, were looking hard at the conglomeration of furniture, rickety tables and torn curtains, and some were grinning. If he noted his guests' behavior, Dick gave no heed."

"'Would you like to hear me play?' he asked suddenly. Almost apologetically he looked at the

> *Californians: 'I know your time is limited.' As he went to the piano with its discolored keys, a chicken ran by. A goat nuzzled him, and a picture frame, empty, fell from a disordered mantle. Octavia Dockery crept by on crutches, to sit on the corner of a sofa. She had spilled hot soup on her foot, she said. Her tired voice trailed away, and Dick's notes rolled out – a sugary waltz, full of trills, runs, and crossing of hands. Catching my eye, he murmured, apropos of nothing: 'I'm a confirmed invalid, but not a menace to society.' Then he resumed, his tongue thrust out a bit, his eyes fixed ahead of him, and he forgot his audience. It was hard to listen without a catch in the throat, and I walked away."*
>
> *"The past pokes a bony finger, cackling wildly to itself at Goat Castle. It is a vast joke, but on whom, or what? For fifty cents, now, you may get in and peer and feel superior, if you can."*

A developer eventually purchased the land, which is now a housing addition, with streets reminiscent of the old home: Glenwood Drive and Dana Road.

Glenburnie has been restored to its original beauty, and is featured on Natchez' Pilgrimage Tour of Homes.

Mammy's Cupboard

One of the first times that my wife and I were driving into Natchez on U.S. 61, we happened to look over to our right and saw something that definitely caught our attention: a thirty-foot-high lady that looked a lot like "Mammy" from that classic old movie *Gone With The Wind*.

Since it was lunchtime, we pulled into the parking lot and walked in a door in the lady's brick skirt... and into an incredible little restaurant. The fare was sandwiches and side-orders. The food was simply delicious – and we ate right there in Mammy's skirt.

The building was so intriguing that we just had to know more about the place... how in the world did this grand woman come to be watching over highway 61?

After doing a little research, we found that the building was erected all the way back in 1940 by Henry Gaude' as a gas

214

station and souvenir shop. The intriguing design was apparently done to pull motorists off the road... just like it did my wife and me. Originally there were three Shell gas pumps out front: one blue, one white, and one yellow.

The structure itself boasts a dining room constructed from cypress beams salvaged from a cotton gin house – since cypress is impervious to insects and rot, Mammy will probably be standing longer that any of us will be alive.

Deserts to Tempt Any Visitor to Mammy's

Mammy's obtained national fame when it was featured in a photograph by Edward Weston, who is known as "The Most Influential American Photographer of the Twentieth Century." He captured the building during its days as a gas station in 1941.

American Heritage Magazine gave a wonderful tribute to the restaurant in its September 1993 issue: *"Mammy's*

Cupboard is an informal monument to one of the most problematic and profound icons of American culture: Mammy. She is a character as powerfully imprinted as the English nanny, a psychological, social, commercial, and racial stereotype who looms large in the American commedia dell'arte of legend and literature—Southern earth mother, source of nutrition, wisdom, comfort, and discipline, cook, adviser, mediator. In such personifications as theater's Ma Rainey and television's Beulah, in literature and film, she remains in myth and memory the most positive of all racial stereotypes."

All I can say is that Mammy's Cupboard is a delightful place to drop in for lunch. The food is delicious – we've eaten there many, many times since that first visit years ago, and we always drive away satisfied. The service is also worth the trip, because when we're there we feel like we're among friends, not just strangers... the folks there always make you feel welcome.

Mammy's Cupboard
555 Hwy 61 S
Natchez, MS 39120
601.445.8957

Miss Nellie's House

One of Natchez' famous – or perhaps infamous – institutions shut its doors well over a decade ago. Although the building still stands, you'll never see a historical marker out front, it's not found on any tourist map of the city, nor will you ever see it featured as one of the beautiful Pilgrimage homes.

In fact, many people are happy that it is slowly fading into obscurity. You see, for over sixty years, a nondescript, white house with red awnings was the illicit place of business known as "Nellie Jackson's."

Nellie was an African-American woman born in Wilkinson County on August 3, 1902. In 1921, she bought the white house. Within ten years, she had moved several young ladies in, operating the place as a bordello – a house of ill repute.

Gentlemen callers would go to the back door of the house where they could discreetly enter and take a seat at the kitchen table. Nellie's girls would parade out and join the men, and before long, match-ups would be made and a little business would be transacted. There was a girl for every gentleman's preference – Black, White, or Asian – but the girls had two things in common: they conducted themselves as ladies, and they were all strikingly beautiful. For a price as high as seventy-five dollars, a caller could get a date with one of these girls for an hour.

Miss Nellie only had a few rules, but they were strictly enforced: 1) all callers had to behave as gentlemen; 2) business between the men and the ladies of the house had to be transacted before midnight; and 3) no drunks were allowed – anyone who showed up at the door intoxicated earned a swift ride downtown in a police cruiser.

Especially during the mid-1900s, anyone in town could give you directions to Miss Nellie's house... even a policeman on the street corner. Over the years, she had the respect of mayors, aldermen and law enforcement; many say that one of the reasons was that she kept exact records of who came to call on her girls. Some report that she even recorded license plate numbers and took photographs as a kind of insurance against any problems with the city. There is wide speculation as to exactly who might have been a customer at her establishment over the years. Whatever the case, she was a force to be reckoned with in the city of Natchez.

Over a decade ago, the *Alexandria Daily Town Talk* ran an article about Nellie, quoting from an ex-mayor of Natchez. When asked to comment about Miss Nellie and her "house of ill repute," the official's comment was simply, "Every town needs one."

Nellie Jackson was said to be a formidable figure around Natchez. She drove a huge white Lincoln that was sometimes chauffeured, had small French Poodle dogs with her, and at a glance would seem to the casual observer as a wealthy socialite. Like any upstanding citizen in town, her credit was as good as her word.

On one occasion a group of proper Natchez ladies started a campaign to shut Nellie's house down, but the effort was short-lived. Police did arrest her, but during her brief tenure at the police station she was put in a private cell where the door was never closed, and a personal chef made sure that she did not go hungry while waiting for the situation to be cleared up. It was taken care of in short order.

Whether they loved her or hated her, everyone in town knew Miss Nellie and they were all saddened and shocked by her death on July 12, 1990; it was a violent and tragic end to a woman who had become a town icon.

A story in the *Houston Chronicle* on June 22, 1990, gives a portrayal of that fateful summer evening. A young man – a university student – arrived at the house in the wee hours of the morning on July 5th and pounded on the door until he woke Miss Nellie and probably everyone else in the house. Since the hour was so late and the man seemed to be heavily intoxicated, the madam turned him away, insisting that he leave the property. The man went to a nearby gas station in a fit of anger, filled an ice chest with gasoline and returned to take an unthinkable vengeance on Miss Nellie for her inhospitality.

He returned to the house, pounded on the door once again. When Miss Nellie answered he doused her with the gasoline, then struck a match. It had spilled not only on the porch, but on the perpetrator as well, so both the young man and the madam exploded into flames.

Miss Nellie suffered in pain for a week with third-degree burns over her entire body, before finally succumbing to the injuries on July 12th.

Today, the house where that famous lady conducted business for over sixty years is a private residence, so please respect the privacy of the current owners. It wasn't that long ago, however, when gentlemen callers could visit there for an evening with one of Miss Nellie's lovely ladies.

The Potential Power of Muscadine Wine

Some studies say that it prevents and treats Coronary Heart Disease, Allergies, Parkinson's, Alzheimer's, Rheumatoid Arthritis, Cardiovascular Disease, Heart Disease, Cataracts, Immune System Decline, and Cancer... to name but a few dreaded diseases. What is this miracle cure, and why isn't it part of the medicinal regiment of every doctor in America? Well, to find the answers to those questions you don't have to go much further than the Old South Winery in Natchez.

While they are not making a single healing claim, they do provide products from the Muscadine grape... and the evidence for Muscadine is mounting in its favor. Recent studies have found that Muscadine grapes and products made from them

220

contain more resveratrol and other antioxidants than any other types of grapes. Muscadine grapes contain antioxidants in skins, seed, pulp, juice and wine – just like you'll find at the Old South Winery. Dr. Arthur Klatsky, chief of the Division of Cardiology at the Oakland-based Kaiser Permanente Medical group monitored 8,000 people for 10 years. The results – published in *Alcohol and Mortality: A New, Prospective Kaiser Permanente Study, Annals of Internal Medicine, 117, 1992* – showed that people who drink one or two glasses of wine per day live longer and are less likely to die from any disease than either abstainers or heavy drinkers.

While researching this book, I did a web search on the benefits of Muscadine wine – the results were apparently undeniable. Most every health resource touted the benefits of drinking a glass of wine every day, but Muscadine wine goes even further. It contains a high level and unique variety of antioxidants that appears to boost the immune system. As I was reading through all this research, it occurred to me that when I told the story I had to be careful to point out that I'm not a physician, and you should do your own digging before believing any claims that anyone might make. That said, I enjoyed tasting their wines – the potential health benefits made the visit even better. The wine was delicious, and I'd have to put our visit to the Old South Winery in the win column. As we drove away, I had a case of their wine in the back of the car.

Does the Muscadine grapes heal arthritis, cancer and such? To be honest, I have absolutely no idea. At this point in my life, though, I'm willing to take a few chances, and a bit of wine from the Old South Winery might be just the thing.

Old South Winery
65 South Concord Ave.
Natchez, MS 39120
601.445.9924
www.oldsouthwinery.com

The Battle of the Hoopskirts

There are probably as many ways to tell this story as there are stars in the sky on a clear Natchez evening, but rest assured that any slights in this particular account are completely unintentional. It is a fascinating tale of a conflict that took place in town that may have caused more controversy than all the years of the war against the Northern states put together.

This is the story of the Natchez Pilgrimage; first it saved the town, then ripped it in two, and then rose once again to become an icon of the American south. As the storytellers might say, it all started back in the 1920s…

The majestic city on the bluff was on the brink of ruin. The bustling riverfront that was Natchez Under-the-Hill had dwindled down to a few old buildings – the river had claimed the rest. Ships no longer docked there and the name "Natchez" was slowly slipping into obscurity.

The city had managed to escape the ravages of the Civil

222

War, but in 1908 an invader came that would prove to be much more destructive than the Northern soldiers... the boll weevil.

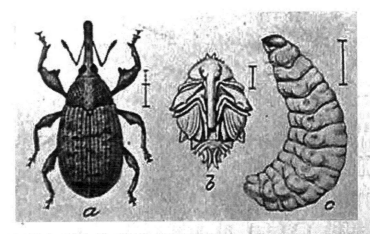

The cotton boll weevil: *a*, adult beetle; *b*, pupa; *c*, larva—enlarged. (From Farmers' Bulletin No. 120, United States Department of Agriculture.)

This little devil crossed the Rio Grande near Brownsville, Texas to enter the United States from Mexico in 1892, and proceeded to spread itself across the American South.

The boll weevil is an unbelievably destructive little beastie when it comes to cotton. They find their way into the cotton fields from early spring through summer, and they start to feed on the immature cotton bolls. The female of the species lays about 200 eggs over the period of two weeks, and in the course of doing so, leaves them on tiny cuts in the cotton flower bud. The eggs hatch in only a few days' time, and the larvae wake up feeding on the cotton for about a week when they enter the pupil stage. They wake up from that in another week, and the cycle of life starts all over again for the boll weevil – all the while decimating the cotton crops. The entire process takes about three weeks; under prime growth conditions, up to ten generations of these little beasties can be produced during a

223

season.

It doesn't take a mathematician to see that only one boll weevil could produce 200 eggs, each of which could produce another 200 eggs making 40,000 more of the critters, which would mean that the next generation would have 8,000,000 of them... and there would be another potential seven generations during a growing season. To the cotton economy of Natchez, the boll weevil was as destructive as one of the Biblical plagues on Egypt.

What the boll weevil didn't do to the cotton crops of the plantation owners, years of over-planting did; the prestegious families that had once ruled the Natchez social scene slowly slid into poverty.

The high and mighty of the city were forced to take whatever menial jobs that could be found. The meager payments that could be made on the mansions were accepted by the banks as a token that was marginally better than eviction. After all, having someone living in a home would help preserve it, should it ever be viable real estate in the future.

Many of the old houses were falling into ruin; the families could not afford to heat the houses in the cold of winter, or do the repairs as needed throughout the year.

As Natchez slowly deteriorated, the entire nation fell into a depression. On October 29, 1929, the date that would become known as "Black Tuesday," the country slid into an economic abyss.

Things looked as bleak for the city on the bluff as they did for any town in America... until something interesting happened in 1931 that would change Natchez forever. Some claim that it was just a fortuitous coincidence, while others see it as the very hand of God intervening to revive the city.

In the early 1930s there was a revival of the garden movement in America – beautiful home gardens became the fashion of the day, and ladies joined Garden Clubs in cities across the nation that were founded to promote the new fad.

The Natchez Garden Club, a group of ladies committed to the beautification of the city even in its declining state, arranged for the Mississippi Federation of Garden Clubs to hold its annual meeting in Natchez in 1931.

It seemed like a natural fit – several of the old city gardens were scheduled to be on display for the Federation, but suddenly tragedy struck. Weeks before the meeting, Mother Nature threw a curve ball to the city of Natchez, and there was a winter storm that brought a hard freeze to the city on the bluff.

Many plants died, and some went back into hibernation; the gardens that were the showplaces of the city quickly withered into ruin. The plans had already been made, however, and could not be stopped. The ladies from around the State descended on the city of Natchez.

There must have been a feeling of panic in the Natchez Garden Club, because there was nothing to show the visitors… until someone thought of the backbone of the city – its stately old homes.

Various owners were quickly persuaded to open their homes for tours. The ladies of the Mississippi Federation of Garden Clubs were treated to old family stories about how the majestic household mirrors were saved during the Civil War, or how the family china had survived for generations to grace the tables during the tours.

In a nutshell, the tours were a hit beyond anything that the Natchez Garden Club could have expected. Nobody seemed to notice the cracked plaster or crinkled wallpaper – or at least the deficiencies were never mentioned. The visitors only saw the majesty of the old homes, and the pride of the people showing them.

Enter a woman named Katherine Grafton Miller, the owner of a house named Hope Farm, and the President of the Natchez Garden Club. The author Harnett T. Kane described her as follows: "She has the deceptively easy charm of the old time Southern belle, together with a rigid determination to get what she wants.

She was, and still is, a dramatic lady, who deals in large things, frets over trifles, hates routine and drives everybody, including herself, close to a breakdown. She talks faster than anyone I ever met, including Tallulah; once I counted that, in a five minute period, she took up and settled the United Nations, ways to prepare shrimp gumbo, the French Quarter of New Orleans, and women who smoke too much (including herself).

You will get ten opinions about her in Natchez, none the same, ranging from unlimited enthusiasm to spluttering resentment. One woman described her by saying that she is more full of ideas than of anything else, fifteen to a minute – thirteen of them ridiculous, and two of them brilliant, but the problem is telling the last two from the rest."

Mrs. Miller saw the success of the home tours that year, and envisioned a historic pilgrimage that would bring flocks of visitors to town. The Natchez Garden Club adopted the idea for a "pilgrimage of homes," and set out to bring their plans to fruition. The ladies called on many of the homeowners, and some were skeptical, if not downright apprehensive. After all, strangers would be traipsing through their homes for a week – who could know what mischief might come from that?

The ladies were persuasive, though, and the plans were finalized. As the next April approached, all the efforts came together. The ladies had sent letters to garden clubs around the country, advertised in newspapers and magazines, and had stretched the boundaries of their experience with publicity.

Old-fashioned dresses with hoopskirts were made for the guides who would show the houses, and the entire town seemed to take in a nervous breath as the time for the Pilgrimage approached.

Something wonderful happened next – people came. They arrived by car, train and bus, all intent on experiencing the

226

majesty of Natchez. Not only did they tour the homes, but they took in the full experience of the city. Every business was overrun with customers; shopkeepers and clerks worked double shifts, restaurateurs had chefs and the waitstaff working overtime. Suddenly there wasn't a person in town who thought that the Pilgrimage was a bad idea. Even it's most vehement detractors fell in line. The first Natchez Pilgrimage was a rousing success.

The homeowners on the tour were allocated a few hundred dollars for their trouble, and with the plight of some of them, you might have thought it to be a fortune. Everyone was happy with the tour of homes and immediately began making plans for the next year.

The Pilgrimage in the spring continued to grow over the next few years, and everyone got in on the action. The entire city prospered in ways that it hadn't since the little devil Boll Weevil had infected the cotton crops. Suddenly visitors were coming to Natchez, and they were leaving their money there at restaurants, gas stations, antique stores, hotels and inns.

A formal Confederate Ball was added to the Pilgrimage festivities, along with a candlelight dance and several other revelries to celebrate the occasion. Pilgrimage continued to grow...

...which may be where the problem started. There's an old saying that is sad but true: money changes everything. Some say that the battle of the hoopskirts began over how much the individual houses were getting paid; others contend that it had to do with the way that the tour homes were selected, and there are several more stories. No matter what the final straw was, however, the outcome ripped the city of Natchez in half.

Katherine Miller had been staying in Vicksburg during this time to help them organize a celebration for the descendants of the famous battle there. When she returned home, she discovered that her supporters had split off from the Natchez Garden Club and formed a new association: the Pilgrimage

Garden Club.

The city that had been united by the historic home tours now had two garden clubs, and two different Pilgrimages. Everything was cordial at first, even if the smiles on the ladies' faces were a little forced. There were two Confederate Balls, two Kings and two queens, and somehow the city survived.

Relations became strained, and the battle of the hoopskirts was on. A person in town was judged by the company that they kept. Heaven forbid, if you were seen having lunch with someone who supported the opposing club, you risked being ostracized from your own circle of friends.

During times when the two Pilgrimages overlapped there was a fierce competition – "Tour our homes, not theirs!" became the battle cry of the day. One garden club took the other to court, and countersuits were filed in response. Local judges not only had wives involved in the process, but had to exist in the town themselves, so rulings were made and then rescinded, and were finally referred to justices in another city.

The ladies of the garden clubs were in a full-scale war. The Irish author Brendan Behan once said, "There's no such thing as bad publicity," and he was right. The conflict between the two clubs hit the press around the country, and people continued to flock to Natchez to see what all the fuss was about.

This "battle of the hoopskirts" became downright nasty, and it is a period of Natchez history that most people don't want to remember. There is, however, a very happy ending to the tale.

Pilgrimage was suspended during the World War II years, but in 1947 peace had broken out around the globe, and also in the city of Natchez. Representatives from both garden clubs sat down and worked out a plan to benefit the city, while still preserving the integrity of both clubs.

The Pilgrimage would be divided and shared. Each garden club would have a king and queen, with one club's serving for

228

the first half, and the other's for the second half. Both clubs would work together to promote the Pilgrimage, and hopefully the town would prosper. During the pageant that first year, Mrs. Melchior Beltzhoover, president of the Pilgrimage Garden Club, bowed on stage to Mrs. Homer Whittington, president of the Natchez Garden Club, who bowed back. The two shook hands and the pageant ensued.

The Historic Natchez Pageant

And prosper the town did. The crowds continued to flock to Natchez, as they still do. Today there is a Spring Pilgrimage and a Fall Pilgrimage, and many of the stately old homes are open to the city's visitors. The battle of the hoopskirts is long passed, but the legacy of the ladies who envisioned the home tours continues to live on, while the damage done by the boll weevil has been buried in Natchez history forever.

And in Closing...

It is incredibly hard to write this chapter – it's a lot like leaving Natchez after a visit there, driving across the Mississippi River bridge, looking back at the city on the bluff in the rearview mirror.

Whether you realize it or not, at that moment your mind is already planning a return visit. After all, if you've been to the Spring Pilgrimage, then you simply must return for Fall – there are still houses to see.

With each trip you'll hear about restaurants that you haven't been able to visit yet, or shops that you haven't browsed through.

Some people find a favorite place to stay and come back time and time again, while others seek out different lodging every trip for a different Natchez experience – and the city does have may hotels, inns, and B&Bs. A person would never tire of the variety.

It would be impossible to fully explore and experience Natchez. It's a city of deep history and mystery... one that a person could fall in love with, in a romance that could last a lifetime.

Index